Transform Your Business

Cheeky Monkey
Nina Dar

Hodder Education

338 Euston Road, London NW1 3BH.

Hodder Education is an Hachette UK company

First published in UK 2011 by Hodder Education.

This edition published 2011.

Copyright © 2011 Nina Dar

British Library Cataloguing in Publication Data: a catalogue record for this title is available from the British Library.

10 9 8 7 6 5 4 3 2 1

www.hoddereducation.co.uk

Typeset by Cenveo Publisher Services.

Printed in Great Britain by CPI Cox & Wyman, Reading.

Also available in ebook

Do what you love. Love what you do.

If you don't this book won't mean what it should to you.

Delivering business transformation takes passion.

Passion comes from love. Let love be an inspiration.

Thank you

You don't get to do the things I do without having brilliant people around you: Yasmin, Dani, Phil, Mickey, Saira, Barry, Sofia, Hollie, Ben, Kenny, the Carter Family, Jane, Pete, Sarah, Nick and Tanya – you are all brilliant, thank you for your unfaltering support no matter how much of a diva I am.

I have the mum and dad everyone wants. I am so lucky they are mine, they are my rock and finally get to see what it is I do with all my time.

The Desperate Housewives of Rectory Gardens and the boys in East Stand Level 3, Aisle 306, Row A, City of Manchester Stadium (home of MCFC) who keep me smiling.

Martin, Kevin, Julian, Paul, Iain and Marc, thanks for putting up with my Dictaphone. The stories are fab.

Mital Daya the Cheeky Monkey illustrator and one of the nicest guys you will ever meet.

Special thanks to all the amazing people we get to work with and the pioneers of change everywhere.

Cover image credits

Front cover: © Mital Daya

Back cover: © Jakub Semeniuk/iStockphoto.com, © Royalty-Free/Corbis, © agencyby/iStockphoto.com, © Andy Cook/iStockphoto.com, © Christopher Ewing/iStockphoto.com, © zebicho - Fotolia.com, © Geoffrey Holman/iStockphoto.com, © Photodisc/Getty Images, © James C. Pruitt/iStockphoto.com, © Mohamed Saber - Fotolia.com

Contents

Introduction

You know you need or want to do something to transform your business but don't know where to start? This book is for you.

Wikipedia definition – business transformation

Business transformation is a key executive management initiative that attempts to align People, Process and Technology initiatives of an organization more closely with its business strategy and vision to support and help innovate new business strategies and meet long-term objectives.

Cheeky Monkey definition – business transformation

Business transformation is about joining the dots. It is knowing what you want your business to achieve tomorrow while being honest about what it is achieving today. It is a map that everyone in the business can read, so they can see what they are accountable for and what the rules are that dictate if they have got there or not.

Size and status does not matter here. If you own a business, you have been trusted to run a business for someone else or you are a magical component of a much larger sum of parts in a corporation, you will get something out of this book.

In this book there are 99 steps that will transform your business. There is a mixture of science and magic. I love the inspirational business books that talk to our inner creative warrior (there is some of that) but I see the need for some hard stuff that genuinely provides business substance and sustainable change, written in a way that doesn't mean you need an army of consultants on site to figure it out (so there is some of that too).

Some provide an instant hit and take no time at all. Others are more complicated – they will take some thought and planning, and maybe some help along the way. With the book comes an invitation to work with us directly via www.cheeky-monkey.co/connect and we will take this journey with you should you wish. If you are a loner, it will work just the same, it just may not be as much fun.

Cheeky Monkey philosophy:

▶ We say what no one wants to hear but everyone wants to say.
▶ We think, do and say the unthinkable for the management team.
▶ We deliver business benefits that go way beyond the project headlines.
▶ We have a 100% fearless focus on business transformation for the better and the bottom line.
▶ We are challenging, probing, enabling, empowering.
▶ We are unstuffy, unusual, quirky and unafraid to have fun!

The Way of the Monkey is our method and is how this book is structured – I take you through the same process I would if I was part of your team.

Business transformation is not a project, it is a management initiative that will result in you choosing projects, or even a programme of projects, that will deliver the change you need for your transformation strategy. All will become clear.

There are a lucky seven component parts in The Way of the Monkey (and in this book):

1 The art of the possible

The opportunity to put everything out there, create your own blueprint, look at where you are now with honesty and dream about where you want to be.

2 The end

Taking your blueprint and being clear about where you want to be tomorrow. Seeing the gaps between that and what exists today. What you have and what difference that makes to where you want to be.

3 The story

More than just the facts, the reason to believe that will engage your whole work force, whether that is one person or 1,000 people. Communication and kicking the whole thing off, the bit that is going to give everyone 20:20 transformation vision and save so much heartache later.

4 Doing it and delivering it

More people can talk about delivering transformation than have actually successfully delivered it! It is easy to get lost in transformation; one or two projects start to drift, people get bored, the deliverables don't seem to be as expected and things just change. This section is all about keeping it real and getting the job done.

5 Looking, learning and moving on

Business transformation is a management initiative, a cycle, always striving to improve and take the next step. This is about creating a loop that continually looks back so you can continue to move forward.

6 Science

Science is a tool bag for you to dip in and out of as you see the need. It is difficult to guess what will help you in your journey without us talking so these are a selection of tools that I use constantly, regardless of company size or area of expertise, and they produce great results every time. They are simple but effective and all result in helping you remove noise and gain clarity.

7 Magic

Cheeky Monkey delivers a human approach to innovation and change. We believe that if you don't get it right with your people, your transformation will not be successful. People are more complicated than machines and this section is all about understanding that in a way that will make people happier, more creative and hopefully able to enjoy the transformation journey.

You don't need to read the book from start to finish to use it; you can jump in and out depending on what you need. Each of the steps stands on their own and Sections 1–5 form a structure if you want to follow a programme. Science and magic are to dip in and out of, and to provide tools or inspiration as you need them. In each section you will get:

▶ Me facilitating your journey. There are lots of questions to challenge what you are doing along with the instructions of what to do.
▶ Bits of Cheeky Monkey Wisdom which will answer some of the answers to the voices in your head, give you a kick and provide some 'been there done that' advice.
▶ A link to talk to me and the rest of the team at Cheeky Monkey via www.cheeky-monkey.co/connect

Cheeky Monkey is a 21st century family. I have always chosen to work with family and friends – it is the biggest privilege I can imagine, spending everyday surrounded by people that you really love. Our clients and partners are friends too, not in some hippy commune sort of way (before you put the book down and run for the hills), but because we all share a passion for the same things done in the same way – no more complicated than having fun, doing good and making money.

If that sounds like you, join us! We are alive and kicking on all the usual outlets:

Twitter – @wayofthemonkey.co.uk
Facebook – Cheeky Monkey Business Solutions
LinkedIn – Nina Dar
YouTube – Channel PLM

We mix business with pleasure; it's how we ensure a good work–life balance. You're as likely to hear about us discussing football or showing a video from a gig as you will get snippets on the latest business transformation thinking. We are not faceless robots; we have a life and are not ashamed to enjoy and share it.

There is always a story in business transformation. Inspirational leaders are great storytellers, they perform their vision in a way that captivates us and makes us want to be part of that journey. I grew up captivated by my parents' stories of triumph over evil and my dad's determination to make small changes count in the world. Stories make the facts add up because someone has been bothered to join the dots for us – we can see the difference between good and bad in the situation without guessing.

Sprinkled throughout the book are the stories of some friends of Cheeky Monkey who have been there and done that when it comes to business transformation. Listening to someone else's story is worthwhile time out, especially when those people are open and share what it was like for them, the good and the bad, and the learning they are passing on. These stories are moments of truth shared in the hope they will help you reflect on your own story and see the common themes that everyone goes through when delivering change.

Seven very successful storytellers have agreed to be part of the book:

Shaukat Dar – my dad
Julian Hartley – CEO at University Hospital South Manchester (UHSM)
Martin Davies – CEO at Holidaybreak PLC
Kevin Murphy – MD at The Foundry Communications Ltd
Marc Lind – Senior VP Global Marketing at Aras Corporation
Iain Speak and Paul Byrne – Board Directors at Bibby Distribution Ltd

Each of the stories is very different and covers transformation from a variety of angles. Hopefully each one will be inspirational and provide some insights.

They give you proof that the things that I talk about work.

Enough of the chat, now it's time to start. Probably the most commonly asked question is: where do we start?

By understanding the art of the possible.

Section 1
The Art
of the
Possible

CRITIQUING

Step 1

Just keeping up or making things happen

Your business does not need to grow to survive but it does need to continually improve just to keep up. Maintaining your position can be harder than growing. Our environment is constantly changing; managing change is a given which means that companies are in perpetual transition, some by accident and some by design. It doesn't matter if you use the language or not, actively manage change or don't, we are all affected by what is happening around us. For some it's just about being aware and fine-tuning what they offer and how. For others there are wholesale changes. For the smart and knowledgeable there are fantastic opportunities.

The heart is where companies will win and lose this decade. That heart contains the people, processes and technology that will allow the business to perform like an athlete or like a couch potato.

There are specifics that are already happening and will accelerate as the decade moves on:

- ▶ The world economy will remain volatile and chaotic.
- ▶ Competition will be global.
- ▶ Market changes will be fast and unpredictable.
- ▶ Emphasis will be on the ability to deliver change (not manage it).
- ▶ Speed will be important (pace of change and to market).
- ▶ Differentiation will win.
- ▶ Competitive advantage will be about having the knowledge to differentiate, people and networks.
- ▶ Sustainability will be about all resources (natural, human and financial).

JUST KEEPING UP OR MAKING THINGS HAPPEN

IT'S WIDELY ACKNOWLEDGED THAT THERE ARE FOUR DRIVING
FORCES FOR THIS NEXT DECADE.

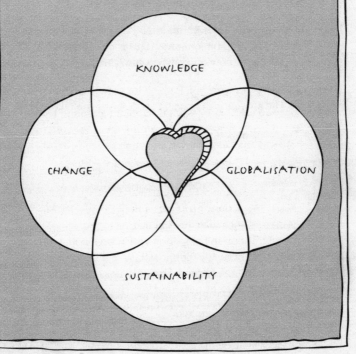

- ▶ Innovation will be continuous and create new business models and venture partnerships.
- ▶ Technology that starts at design phase, delivers information, supports communication, enables e-business transactions and distributed decision-making will underpin business transformation activity.
- ▶ Production processes will integrate lean supply chains with consumer-driven value chains to provide a business-wide value perspective.
- ▶ Organizational structures will be flatter, networked, flexible and demand employee empowerment.
- ▶ Success measures will move towards overall company values, rather than short-term profit targets.

If you are reading this list and thinking 'I might as well throw the towel in now', just hold on a minute. This is not about what you know now; it's about how quickly you can learn.

The process starts here: are you looking for growth or to maintain what you've got? The process is the same, the decisions you take are not.

Take part in the discussion at www.cheeky-monkey.co/connect

Cheeky Monkey Wisdom

Many companies fail because they are successful and can't cope with the growth that success brings. They don't plan for it and when it happens they can't grow the infrastructure of the business quickly enough to cope. For start-ups there is also the role of the entrepreneur, who has to transition from energy-driven go-getter and master of all the business has to offer to letting go and being motivator, trainer, coach and shoulder to cry on for the growing number of employees. Deciding that you are going to grow is not just about winning the business, it's about keeping it.

Step 2

The good

Once you have consciously decided to make business transformation part of your routine there is a tendency to focus on the bad stuff. All the things that don't get done well, the mistakes that have been made, the specifics that need to change. That is tough love for the people who work in the business, who probably know that things need to change but don't need to feel like everything they have done so far hasn't been adequate. That is never the truth anyway.

Start with a positive focus on the good in the business. Involve everyone at this stage and ask them what they think is good about the business. Ask them to tell you why they still get up in the morning and come to work. Ask yourself why you do. Get to the heart of why you and everyone in this business care and what you and they care about.

Take part in the discussion at www.cheeky-monkey.co/connect

Cheeky Monkey Wisdom

The way people see something affects their relationship with it. If you start your transformation with what's wrong, negative emotions are raised instantly. Business transformation is not about making you unrecognizable, it's about improving on what is there. Understanding the good stuff not only raises positive emotions, it makes sure you don't inadvertently change it.

Step 3

....

Treasure the moaning

Knowledge is going to be one of the key drivers this decade and we couldn't be more inundated with information, but that doesn't give us knowledge or the skill of evaluating it so that we can do something with it.

The organizational change pioneer Dr Russell Ackoff (1919–2009) said the content of the human mind can be classified into five categories:

1 **Data:** facts
2 **Information:** data that are processed to be useful; provides answers to 'who', 'what' 'where', and 'when' questions
3 **Knowledge:** application of data and information; answers 'how' questions
4 **Understanding:** appreciation of 'why'
5 **Wisdom:** evaluated understanding

He also said the first four categories deal with the past and only the fifth, wisdom, deals with the future because it incorporates vision and design. With wisdom, people can create the future rather than just grasp the present and past. But achieving wisdom isn't easy; people must move successively through the other categories to get there.

When people moan, complain and are frustrated, their minds go through all five of Dr Russell's categories naturally. Experiment with someone you know and I bet it will go like this:

1 You will hear what was wrong (data).
2 Then how, what, where it was wrong (information).
3 On to what they wanted and how it should have been different (knowledge).

4 Moving into why if it was different it would be better (understanding).

5 Ending with, 'if only (or it would be brilliant if) you could, or this existed, or that happened' (vision).

Best of all, this process is usually emotionally driven, so is less likely to be politically correct. That is gold.

Harvesting knowledge and translating it into a vision is something we all need to practise because there is significant value to be placed on that process.

In this step you need to get people moaning about what you do, the products and services, your business, people, relationships, systems. People might already be doing it; search online and see what they are saying if you don't already know. This is not about being negative: relish the moaning, knowing that knowledge is priceless in your transition.

Take part in the discussion at www.cheeky-monkey.co/connect

Cheeky Monkey Wisdom

Nothing makes people happier than telling you that something is not right but, depending on the culture of the people you are dealing with, you might have to use different techniques to get people to open up. In Asia generally people don't want to upset you and would rather let something slide than tell you why it's wrong, so the process needs to be more focused on continuous improvement, rather than moaning. In Africa there can be a tendency to believe nothing will change anyway, so you may have to navigate the negativity before you get to the knowledge and vision. In the Western world, get a comfy chair; you might be there for some time.

Step 4

Space to dream

Do you daydream? It seems like the ultimate luxury in our frantic space to allow our minds to drift. Yet it can be the most rewarding time you invest. There are lots of people that get into the office early so they can answer emails before the mayhem and buzz of the day begins. We focus so much now on keeping on top of the transactional stuff, when do we think? What effect would it have on you if once or twice a week you used that early morning time just to go somewhere calm and let your mind wander? To think about what you are working on and why? How is it going? Is it how you imagined it would be?

Business transformation has to include some dream time in two parts:

1 You have to have a dream, something that you are aiming for in a space that is not constrained by what you are knee-deep in every day. The only limits in this space are your own and if you are going to work on transformation you need to understand what they are and be critical with yourself about this first.

2 You need space to think, to go through Dr Russell's thought process with the information you are collecting. If you don't, you will have data and maybe some information, but not knowledge, and definitely not vision.

Transformation is about achieving something more, going beyond where you are today. For that to make sense and make a difference, you need head space to think and dream of the possible.

In this step you have to dream. What is it you want to do? What difference will it make? Why are you in this business? What does this mean to you?

Take part in the discussion at www.cheeky-monkey.co/connect

Cheeky Monkey Wisdom

My dream was to establish a business that did serious things but didn't take itself seriously. To provide a sounding board for companies who are sometimes constrained by the four walls they are in. To be a catalyst for change that would keep the British entrepreneurial spirit alive, and to do this with a brand that would endear itself to those who have to deliver the dream. I wanted Cheeky Monkey to be a smack right across the face and then the hug and kiss that made it all worthwhile.

For four out of our six years in business, many people tried to get me to change the company name. I know we could have made more money had I played it safe. That wasn't my dream.

Step 5

....

Connections

The heart in Step 1 links people, process and technology; to be an athlete the connections we make in these three areas are critical. There is a lot of talk about networks. It's one of those mind-blowing topics that as you start joining the dots in your own head it makes perfect sense, but it is an elephant that needs breaking into parts before you have the faintest idea what you can do with it.

The Information Age: Economy, Society & Culture (Vol. I, II & III) by Manuel Castell has inspired my thinking about connections but it is an area that needs to be simplified to allow you to take what's important to you into your thinking.

We already know we can do just about anything anywhere as long as there is the IT structure in place to support it. The flow of activities required can be completely independent of the physical location in which they are carried out and the physical place where the final transaction is done. We can operate virtually.

Globalization has been driving virtual working for some time and we have all been touched by it in some form in our personal lives, if not professional, usually through contact with overseas call centres and online shopping.

This way of working is putting pressure on traditional organizational structures because it forces a more dynamic way of working that matches itself to a virtual team working towards a common goal (which could be short term) rather than a functional department supporting a longer-term business goal (I know that is a huge simplification but just go with it for now).

This is seeing a move away from the traditional form support activities detailed in Porter's value chain (infrastructure, HR, technology, procurement) to an acknowledgement that more than one infrastructure will be considered and there is value in creating connections between infrastructure, people, process and technology across your network.

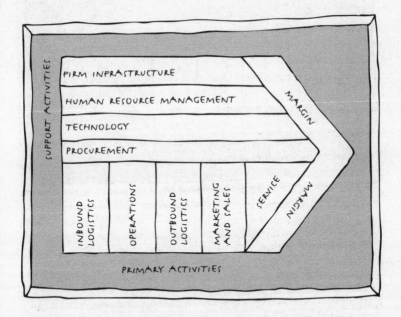

That results in a global value chain, where the flow of activities is based wherever the people are that you need to carry out the activities.

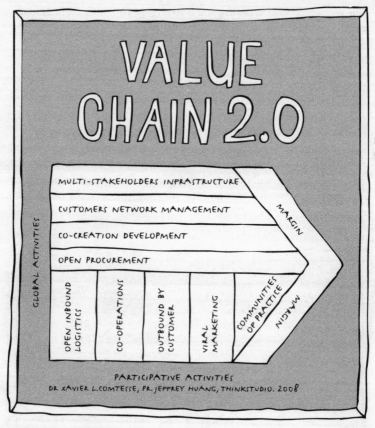

© Dr Xavier L. Corntesse, Professor Jeffrey Huang, ThinkStudio, 2008.

It makes perfect sense: not all the smart people in the world want to work *for* you anymore, but some of them want to work *with* you. You need to tap into as many smart people as possible, regardless of whether they work inside or outside your business because that resource is scarce. By being too regimented over how things happen, you will lose their interest to someone who is more open-minded.

If you work in a heritage business that is going through this transition it is tough. Look at the likes of British Airways and Royal Mail. These are businesses that will not survive without making these connections, but the effects are felt by the employees and challenge the culture that has existed for many years.

The organizational structure starts to change the more connections you focus on:

- flexibility
- interconnectivity
- devolved decision-making and leadership
- employee empowerment
- a flatter hierarchy.

Most businesses are schizophrenic about this transition and it makes it really tough on the people who are on the receiving end of the change. This step is about thinking through the connections you have now, how effective they are and the ones you know you need to make, what pressure that is going to put on how your business is structured today and the culture that exists.

Take part in the discussion at www.cheeky-monkey.co/connect

Cheeky Monkey Wisdom

People don't resist change, they resist badly managed change. Creating the connections you will need to take your business forward may result in fundamental changes to the way your employees work and the culture they are part of. Culture is a complicated area, it is a set of beliefs we identify with. When our interpretation of those beliefs changes (new corporate goals or strategy), we don't automatically change the connection we make with them just because someone has told us it's better. Sometimes we have no option but to stay and ride the change out, even though we don't agree with it. These people can so easily become the disaffected and you need to try hard to ensure that doesn't happen.

It is fascinating to watch Generation Y coming through the workforce. Their culture aligns more with technology than it does with people and process. At face value that may seem so much easier, but it is still people that add the value to your business.

Step 6

The blueprint

The blueprint is the flow of decision-makers, information and activity that exists in every business.

Business transformation looks at all elements of that blueprint to understand where improvements can be made, especially in alignment of people, process and technology, to deliver your dream.

In its simplest form a blueprint has:

- ▶ market (product and somewhere to sell it)
- ▶ process (how you make, deliver and sell it)
- ▶ financials (how much it costs to do it and what you have left).

As companies grow there is a need for more things to go into the blueprint:

- ▶ policies (statements of what you will and won't do)
- ▶ information (compliance and intellectual property)
- ▶ research and development (innovating to keep the business alive)
- ▶ procurement (where all the materials are coming from)
- ▶ new product introduction (delivering innovation to the customer)
- ▶ portfolio management (the lifecycle of your products)
- ▶ marketing (brands and communication)
- ▶ business planning (where we are going)
- ▶ talent management (where our people are).

In addition, the processes get more complicated:

- ▶ integrated business planning
- ▶ idea to market
- ▶ project management
- ▶ supply chain management

- ▶ product lifecycle management
- ▶ sales and operation planning
- ▶ customer relationship management
- ▶ human resources
- ▶ customer service.

Drawing your business blueprint is a must-do. You need to understand the gaps between the here and now, and the dream.

Take part in the discussion at www.cheeky-monkey.co/connect

Cheeky Monkey Wisdom

We have established that business transformation is a basic management principle. You understand your business; you are honest about where you stand today, have a picture of where you are going to go tomorrow and you rack up all your assets to deliver that picture.

The blueprint is a map of what exists today in your business. Don't be tempted to embellish or connect things that aren't really connected today. At this point keep the dream and today in separate places.

Step 7

Be honest about today

We need to do some looking in and out to be able to answer questions and there is no better way to do that than to complete a SWOT (Strengths, Weaknesses, Opportunities and Threats) exercise.

Our willingness to involve everyone (bottom up, top down, inter silo) has led to the over-initiative era. Lots of initiatives and projects exist in every organization I go in to. Many initiatives are not successful and, in many cases, frustration is at an all-time high.

Fear and resistance to change have been replaced with over-initiative numbness and confusion. People are just tired of what it adds to their workload. Guess what? In most companies, silos still exist because they are fundamental to the design of the organizational structure, not because people won't change or don't want to work in a different way!

Matrix management is just a way of formalizing two different approaches to working: functional and project.

Projects were once a vehicle to deliver change outside 'business as usual'. Now they are business as usual.

Think about this when you do your SWOT. How many things are in play? What is good and what isn't? When you look at opportunities think about connections. This is your opportunity to let people release their frustrations and tell you what they are proud of. It has to be about collaboration and better use of what we have got. Think sustainability. It is not just about natural resources and the environment; it is about how we use all resources.

Take part in the discussion at www.cheeky-monkey.co/connect

Cheeky Monkey Wisdom

A SWOT may seem 'old skool' but it is a simple and effective way of uncovering a number of things beyond the headline. Take the opportunity to see how people are interacting, who knows what about things happening outside of your four walls. What do people really think your strengths are? Do they match your view? Can you see the culture that really exists in your business? Is that going to help or hinder your transformation?

Step 8

Give yourself credit

If you have carried out the SWOT exercise, you will have something that resembles a messy wall, with sticky notes and lines and more scribbles on top. Now it's time to give yourself a pat on the back and give yourself some credit for what you do well.

Got that warm glow? Out of that list what do you do better than everyone else?

Understanding what you do better than anyone else is sometimes harder than it sounds. We operate in crowded markets and it can feel like you just do the same as everyone else but yours is better. Why?

It might not be obvious. Is it communication, distribution, sourcing materials, your recipes?

Understanding what you do better makes you focus on the value you add, the thing that you should always keep hold of. The things that sit outside that are opportunities to make connections with people who do that activity better than everyone else.

In this step we are adding clarity to our thinking: looking for a sustainable route through business transformation with the focus on making the best use of what you are good at and being efficient about where someone else could do it better, seeing an opportunity or threat that needs support.

▶ What do you do well now?
▶ What would you need to change to respond to an existing opportunity?
▶ What do you need to change to ensure a threat doesn't take you down?

Take part in the discussion at www.cheeky-monkey.co/connect

Cheeky Monkey Wisdom

Are there weaknesses that you have not looked to change? When you did look to improve them, were your answers a bit flaky? Do you just need to stop doing certain things? Knowing when to stop is a sign of greatness not failure.

Step 9

Sharing won't kill you

Your personal and business networks are priceless when you are re-evaluating where you are and what you should do. Obviously you don't want to tell your competitors what you have planned, but think about all the people who are either in the same boat as you or, even better, have been where you are and have come out the other side (good and bad).

Picking some people for whom there may be mutual benefit from sharing is good for the soul. It's isolating running a business. Getting the opportunity to talk things over, review ideas and brainstorm issues with people who have no ulterior motive, just to look at continuous business improvement, the same as you, is energizing and can help make swift work of what you are trying to do. It cuts out the time you spend wondering if you really have thought of everything.

If your networks are not what they should be, invest some time in this area. People move around frequently and it is easy to lose touch but LinkedIn (www.linkedin.com) is a fantastic tool to help you reconnect with ease and minimum fuss.

To get the best out of these experiences you have to be generous. If you approach it as an opportunity to give something to your network (e.g. share some tools, insights, problems and how you have solved them), you will get so much feedback in return. If you go about this just to get some input for what you want, then you might be better with a consultant.

In this step consider sharing what you have done so far so that you can get feedback from your peers – people whose judgement and experience you value.

Take part in the discussion at www.cheeky-monkey.co/connect

Cheeky Monkey Wisdom

You never know what might come of opening yourself and your work up to a well-chosen network. In addition to the benefit of bouncing ideas around and sharing, you may find interesting partnerships that could blossom and connections that you didn't know existed. The largest companies in the world (with the biggest resource budgets) get together to exchange ideas and concepts on how they are looking to drive their businesses forward. It's not about having the ability to do it from the inside; it's the collaboration that creates the magic.

Step 10

Hit pause ... dream vs need

This section is all about the art of the possible; it's not about having your head in the clouds. You need to be able to link these pieces of work into something that clearly describes:

- ▶ where you want to be
- ▶ what your business has today
- ▶ where the opportunities are
- ▶ what you are good at
- ▶ the connections you could make
- ▶ the threats that might take you off track.

If you see a link, then this is the art of the possible, even if it isn't obvious. For example, we worked with a business in Nigeria that produced and distributed personal care products. One of its core competencies was the distribution network across West Africa. The company diversified into food, white goods and cars (not obvious routes from personal care) with the link always being the distribution network – that is the art of the possible.

If you have real threats that may be putting your business at risk then you need to be clear how the transformation is going to answer those threats en route to delivering the dream. It can feel like you need to deal with the burning platform before anything else. So often the burning platform is not the issue – you need to find the source of the fire. To do this you have to be courageous and clear with your rationale for what you tackle and when.

When you have created the links you should have a map of your business landscape. There might be so much you need to do and stuff that you want to do, you might be thinking 'how do I choose?'

It might even look like everything needs to be done and there is just a mass of conflicting priorities. We need to get rid of some of the noise and generate the 'Aha' moment.

Take part in the discussion at www.cheeky-monkey.co/connect

Cheeky Monkey Wisdom

You only know what you know. Make sure you are keeping in touch with what is going on in the world – you don't need to go through the learning curve that others have done before you. Take a tip from the emerging markets, see the latest thinking and or technology and go straight to it. (Who needs landlines when you can have mobile phone technology...)

STORY 1: LITTLE TRANSFORMATIONS ADD UP TO BIG THINGS

Storyteller: Shaukat Dar

Shaukat was born and raised in Kenya. He started his career in engineering in Kenya then, following a move to the UK, he joined United Biscuits where he worked for over 30 years with responsibility for manufacturing TUC, Digestives, Penguin and Jaffa Cakes. He was involved in the design, build and running of the Chocolate Refinery in Stockport and finally the Mini Bar Cake Factory in Halifax.

Me: How would you define business transformation?

Shaukat: To take something which you believe in and make it happen. Be aware of the world, the way it's moving, aware of the industry, aware of the people and the new direction which you can see, but also new direction which can be directed by the others.

Me: You have been involved in so many business transformations; which are the most memorable for you?

Shaukat: I need to point out that not all transformations need to be big initiatives. When I started work I looked for things I could transform every day, when I finished something I would gear up my mind to think how am I going to bring something new tomorrow?

Me: Like what?

Shaukat: It started from when I was in Kenya studying engineering, they were building a new refinery in Mombasa and I saw there was an opportunity for me.

It was something totally new, working with a consortium, having my own area of responsibility within a much larger programme of work. I started observing and thinking about different things:

▶ the different people and skill sets within the industry
▶ what it meant to work with them
▶ the politics – how the government, the industrialists and the working people interacted together.

My strengths were in the technical arena. By observing the managers I was picking up new skills all the time and using them to go one step further than my managers asked every day. It transformed my skill set and allowed me to move to my next project, construction of a hydroelectric dam in Pakistan.

It was my first huge project: constructing the highest earth-filled dam wall, pre-testing the concrete, creating tunnels to house the turbines. With this project my transformation was focused on people, the impact your management style can have on them and what they deliver for you.

Sadly I couldn't finish it and had to come to the UK. It was the end of '60s beginning of the '70s and the unions ruled. The concept of a union was completely new to me and so was the environment where we had to fight for everything, I had worked in harsh environments (Pakistan is not for wimps) but this was different. Race and background mattered and I had to fight just to be accepted.

That was a very personal transformation. I had to rise above the negativity, forget the fact that none of my skills were recognized and start all over again to gain some understanding of this new world and learn some new skills. I started as a biscuit packer at United Biscuits and decided to learn everything about how factories operated in the UK.

I went back to school. I worked during the night and studied during the daytime. That gave me an insight into management theory, what management was all about and in practice I could see it happening in front of me. I soon recognized that my thoughts and my understanding of industry were taking my mind back to where I was at the refinery, observing:

- the different people and skills sets within the industry
- what it meant to work with them
- the politics – how the government, the industrialists and the working people interacted together.

And also that I was bored packing biscuits!

Within my own structure I tried to promote what I believed at that time. I looked for opportunities to take the industry I worked within beyond what it was doing currently.

One of the hardest things to do was to try and convince people around me that's the way we should be going. At every stage I encountered problems; even the smallest change was always challenged.

Me: So are you saying that even with the small things, when you are not perhaps in a position of authority, transformation is still about achieving the next part of excellence, striving for the next thing that will make a difference?

Shaukat: It is you should never stop.

When you're not in a position of authority then you have to fight for it all the time. And when you're having to fight for it all the time, every time you win adds a little more experience to your thoughts which gives you the courage to keep doing what you are doing.

Me: So are you saying then that you can be a transformational person not necessarily in charge of a transformation programme?

Shaukat: Yes. Once you start to make an impact (be it small) in the areas which others regarded as comfortable then your acceptance within that role becomes easier. So once your acceptance within that role becomes easier then you are stepping into having some authority. Once you have authority within your own control then you can accelerate that process.

Me: Is that what happened to you?

Shaukat: Yes. I progressed through the ranks and eventually my industry knowledge, my awareness of what was happening in the world externally and my authority all came together when we started to look at changing the way we made biscuits.

Me: When was this?

Shaukat: This was in the late '70s.

Biscuits were manufactured on lines that were heavily reliant on the expertise of people. Instructions would be issued on a daily basis verbally through a chain of command. Problems would be solved daily the same way. There were people around the industry who became experts, so-called experts because they were the people who actually went around and gave those verbal commands. This is where the supervisor, the first-line supervisors came into being and then there were various structures within the organizations.

Things like making sure the consistency was right, the temperature was right, this is where the craft came into it.

Me: This was in the world where if you were making biscuits you would be a biscuit maker and that would be a skilled job?

Shaukat: Yes absolutely.

Me: You would not just be on a production line?

Shaukat: There were people just on the line non-skilled and then people who issued them instructions who were skilled biscuit makers.

Me: So what was wrong with this situation?

Shaukat: Well first of all there were only a few people who could develop those skills, you know who became Masters. Generally they were known as Masters; either you became a Master Baker or a Master Technician.

Now it did not necessarily mean that they'd been to school or understood the theory side of it. They had to pick these skills up and mastered them over a period of time to create a product which was acceptable by consumers, by the company itself. They were the backbone of what the industry is today.

Me: Automation was to take away the reliance on the Masters?

Shaukat: Yes. There was always pressure to cut costs. Manning levels at the factory came into focus. It was too expensive to have so many people working each line. It was too expensive to have so many technicians working and it was too expensive to have so many

managers working within the industry. *But* it was too expensive not to have some of those people there as well – they had to be replaced with something.

Automation was the start of it and with automation came a huge reduction in the number of people working, a leap forward in terms of getting the technology to do the job.

This also delivered new skills to the people who were left. It was a huge change.

It was a hard and emotional time. It was an industry that employed a lot of people.

When you are responsible for something like that, you do think 'how am I going to drive this? How am I going to achieve this?' Against the background of the political things, other people's interventions and the emotion of it all, when you are not in it and you are looking at it, then you can do what needs to be done.

Personal drive plays a huge role. I didn't get paid for a lot for what I did but that is not what I'm about. What I'm about is, is to be able to make a change for myself, for the company and the rest of the world around me. I just could not accept, sit there every day, doing my job and say 'That's what I'm about, this is what I get paid for.' I wasn't about that. And whether people liked it or not, whether people wanted it from me or not, I made it happen. I made it my business to make it happen.

And my success came from the belief that I can make it happen irrespective of the position in the company I held.

Me: Give me one word that sums up your own experience of transformation.

Shaukat: Don't give up.

Me: That's more than one word.

Shaukat: Go for it.

Me: That's more than one word.

Shaukat: Tenacity.

Section 2
The End

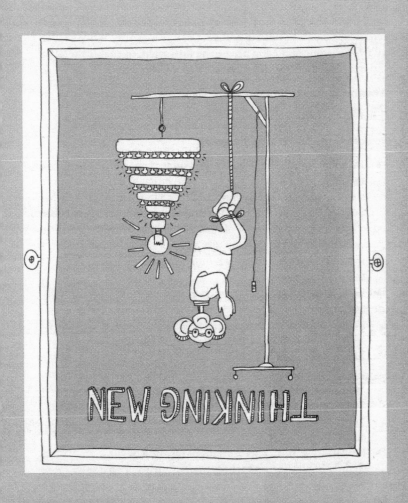

Step 11

Be distracted

Looking at the art of the possible can be quite an intense process. It requires some free thinking and a lot of navel gazing. While that is all fresh in your mind you need to be distracted, to enable the 'Aha' moment, the moment of brilliance that always comes.

There is science behind this logic. There are neuroscientists that study the 'Aha' moment. The following is taken from a book called *Your Brain at Work* by Dr David Rock, who has come up with four things you can do get more 'Aha' moments:

▶ **Be quiet.** Insights tend to involve connections between a small numbers of neurons in the brain; the problem is we only notice them above our baseline noise. We tend to notice insights when our overall activity level in the brain is low. This happens when we're not putting in a lot of mental effort, when we're focusing on something repetitive, or just generally more relaxed as we are when we wake up. Insights require a quiet mind, because they themselves are quiet.

▶ **Look inwards.** Our attention at any moment can be externally focused, like on these words, or internally focused, like on an image you might see in your mind's eye activated by a word. We tend to flick between these two states all the time. When people have insights, they are 'mind wandering', which is like a form of daydreaming. They are not focused externally on the problem. So insights are more likely when you can look inside yourself and not focus on the outside world. When you feel safe enough to 'reflect' on deeper thoughts and not worry about what's going on around you for a moment.

▶ **Be slightly happy.** There is a lot of research to show that being slightly happy, versus slightly anxious, helps people solve more problems and be more creative generally. When people are happy they are more likely to notice a wider range of information, than when they are anxious and more 'tunnel visioned'.

▶ **Don't make an effort.** If you want insights you need to stop trying to solve a problem. The reason for this is that usually insights happen because we become stuck at an impasse. The impasse tends to involve a small set of solutions that we have become fixed on. The more we work on this same wrong solution, the more we prime the brain for that solution and the harder it is to think of new ideas. It's like changing traffic on the freeway – we have to stop the traffic going one way before it can go another. In the brain, wrong solutions push out the right ones.

Try them all and see what works for you. Realize though, sometimes there is no single earth-shattering 'Aha' moment, just a serene sense of confirmation that you are on the right path.

Take part in the discussion at www.cheeky-monkey.co/connect

Cheeky Monkey Wisdom

My 'Aha' moments come from ironing, cleaning, swimming or first thing in the morning in that haze where I am waking up. These are not conscious moments for me; I just always get to the point of being so tired of thinking about something, I need to do something that will stop the thinking process. I always have a stack of ironing or cleaning overdue and am guilt-ridden for not doing enough exercise – it's the icing on the cake that they have a bonus outcome.

Step 12

Picture the end

With your mind at peace and 'Aha' moment in the bag, have a go at the following three questions.

- ▶ Imagine you are at the post-project party. What are you drinking to?
- ▶ You are on the front page of the *Financial Times* today. What does the headline say?
- ▶ What are you going to tell your mum that you have done?

The answer to the first question is about what this means to you, the second what it means to the world and the third the ability to explain it in a way that makes sense.

From this we will get your instinctive view on what you are trying to do; importantly, it also serves as a barometer of your ambition and your ego.

Get these statements posted up on the wall. Is there a relationship between how you picture the end and the work we created in the art of the possible?

Yes? Brilliant! Our map is starting to take shape. No? Where has this end come from then? What is going on? Do you need to revisit the art of the possible or do you need to get your head out of the clouds?

Take part in the discussion at www.cheeky-monkey.co/connect

Step 13

Do nothing

Less is more. In this time of over-initiative syndrome we need to be absolutely clear on the 'why'. You have your headlines, now we need to spend some time tracking back from the point of success.

Can you have the headline by just tidying up? If you tidy some things up (following processes already in place, using existing technology to its capacity, getting rid of people who make life harder than it needs to be), how much of the noise disappears?

Take part in the discussion at www.cheeky-monkey.co/connect

Cheeky Monkey Wisdom

People are much happier to spend time, energy and effort in talking about a new project or initiative than they are fixing the horrible issues that have been around for ages but are messy. Some days you just need to put your rubber gloves on and clean up.

Step 14

Make it relevant

We are all in business to make money. Even charitable organizations employ people who know how to make money because without it they can't do good. The objective of all businesses is to provide a product or service for more money than it has cost to make or deliver it and get someone to buy it more than once. You can be brilliant at making or delivering something, but if your customer doesn't want it you are sunk.

What we need to know now is whether your changes will give your customer something that strongly influences him or her to choose your product or service.

Look at the work you have done to date. Where is the route to the customer? Highlight each time some value is created and why it influences them in choosing your product. If there is no value to the customer, BIN IT.

Knowing that this value will strongly influence them in choosing your product is not enough in these tough times. How big is that market? More to the point, what is it worth? Is it enough to sustain the growth you need? Bluntly, is it worth bothering?

This is not a 'glass half empty' statement, it is a challenge that requires you show why you love your business and come back with a hundred reasons why it is worth bothering. Be disciplined enough to go through each product or service, keeping those that you know make sense, for example:

▶ niche market high margin (we are specialists)
▶ new entry to new market (you have spotted a gap you can deliver in)
▶ me too product or service (done better or cheaper)
▶ new entry in existing market (exciting a customer base who already know and love you)

Bin those that just don't, for example:

- niche market low margin (not specialists)
- me too product or service (not done better or cheaper)
- you know where I am going with this…

Take part in the discussion at www.cheeky-monkey.co/connect

Cheeky Monkey Wisdom

We have delivered a large number of new product development (NPD) project kick-off meetings. At the start of each meeting we ask a simple question that seems to baffle the group every time: 'how will we win in the market with this?' There is always so much noise that you have to be able to focus on what is important. The consumer still is king and queen (and increasingly prince and princess).

Step 15

You are not an island

I said at the start of the book that business transformation needs to be reconciled at the top of the organization. Size can make all the difference to that statement: you may be at the top of your bit in a big corporation or you may be at the top of an SME or it might just be you. Whichever applies, the real questions are:

1 Are you the ultimate decision-maker?
2 Do you hold the key to people and money?
3 Where are you in the food chain? Do people feed off you, you off them or both?

Fast forward and run this scenario in your head: who needs to be involved before this goes too far?

Remember this is about alignment, connections and collaboration. You should not be an island. Business transformation is not about you winning, it's about the business winning.

Take part in the discussion at www.cheeky-monkey.co/connect

Cheeky Monkey Wisdom

Frustration and ambition are two main drivers for people taking charge of transformation and going for it. It is the most soul-destroying position to be in when you realize the hard work and effort have no support. You may not know everything that is going on in your business if you are not the person at the top. Save yourself the heartache – find out before you start. You never know what you might discover.

Step 16

Don't talk yourself out of it

At this point don't talk yourself out of it or water down what you have done because of the fear of putting yourself out there. Self-doubt has a horrible habit of creeping in at just the wrong time; if you want to transform your business you need to move past that to do a really good job of hiding it. It helps to exude quiet confidence – don't shout from the rafters just yet, not because you haven't got something worthy to shout about, but because from this point on it's all about engagement.

Being distracted by other pressing commitments is fear wrapped up in avoidance. Talking about business transformation is worth nothing until you do it.

Take part in the discussion at www.cheeky-monkey.co/connect

Cheeky Monkey Wisdom

I have been through Sections 1 and 2 with companies who are so pleased that we have finally established what the business is all about and the direction it should take. We go to the pub, celebrate, pat ourselves on the back and go back to the office. At that point a mixture of fear and other commitments (avoidance) creep in and the momentum is lost. You can't transform your business without taking action.

STORY 2: WHEN TRANSFORMATION IS ABOUT LIFE AND DEATH

Storyteller: Julian Hartley, CEO, University Hospital of South Manchester

Julian started his career in the NHS as a general management trainee working in the north-east of England. Following his training, he worked in a number of NHS management posts in Middlesborough, Durham and Newcastle working at hospital, health authority and regional levels. His first Board Director appointment was at North Tees and Hartlepool NHS Trust where he was responsible for planning, operations and strategy.

After two years in this post, Julian moved across the Pennines to take up his first Chief Executive post at Tameside and Glossop PCT. He led the PCT for three years during which time he took it to three-star status, developed new Primary Care Centres and managed the PCT's involvement in the Shipman inquiry. Julian stayed in the north-west to move to his previous position as Chief Executive at Blackpool, Fylde and Wyre Hospitals NHS Foundation Trust. He also chairs the North West Leadership Academy which is developing NHS leaders across the region.

Me: How would you define business transformation?

Julian: It means to me, moving to really high performance, characterized by what I describe as deep employee engagement, which is when everyone that works in the organization has a sort of deep and clear understanding of what they're about and how what they do every day is connected to the goals of the organization. That the management and leadership style in that organization has the fundamental principles of great communication, continuous improvement, recognition and an enlightened management style which is easily tested and monitored throughout the organization.

So ultimately you're driving high performance through engagement which ultimately changes the culture of the organization and transforms the business.

Me: Is that what you have done here?

Julian: That's been our approach here at UHSM to tackle some really difficult issues because I don't think you can transform a business, a healthcare organization without attending to the cultural and employee engagement issues. What people think of the place, what they think of their job, what they think of where they work, what they think of their colleagues, how they behave, how they interact. All of those things matter hugely. If you don't deal with those or you don't understand what's going on with those you can't take the performance of the business to a sort of transformational level.

Me: When did you start your transformation here?

Julian: Well I'd probably say from the point that I walked through the door as interim Chief Exec. (I wasn't Chief Exec until three months later.) When I arrived the first thing I did was write to a whole range of staff and introduce myself and then asked them what they thought the top three challenges for the organization were.

What was really interesting was, I got loads of replies and there was quite a lot of commonality in the responses:

▶ We don't know what's going on.
▶ We feel it's top-down performance driven sometimes to the point of management bullying.
▶ We don't have a sense of the vision for the organization.

- There's a real lack of clinical engagement, frontline clinicians and doctors and nurses feeling part of the organization and a separation between management and clinicians.

Those were some of the key themes that came through as well as a lot of operational problems, frustrations and difficulties, and that came through loud and clear.

So what that gave me was a strong sense of what people were thinking and feeling which then when I did my induction and met people on a one-to-one [basis] I was able to use the feedback that they'd given me to structure the conversation.

So before they/I even walked through the door I had a sense of what their issues were. That was going to help me engage with them and I did an awful lot of that because I think the first part of transformation is people understanding what the Chief Executive's about and wanting to know that they're going to be listened to and that there's at least a shared understanding of what the problems are.

That's the first step to share and agree what the big issues are. We then formalized that into a whole series of focus groups and engagement events with different groups of staff where I got the chance to be in a room full of people and get them talking about issues and frustrations and so on. We explored what the top three challenges were. What are the behaviours that need to change? And what kind of organization do we want this to be?

Everyone got quite revved up about that which was great so we got a lot of activity in terms of flipcharts and ideas and post-its. Lots of physical activity going on in terms of shaping that and the process that led to over the space of the first three or four months. It led to the development of the South Manchester Way which is very much a statement of what we're about. At the heart of it which isn't a surprise but needs saying and needs repeating is patient care's at the heart of all we do. Supported by the other components of the South Manchester Way which are about how we behave towards each other:

- Patient care is at our heart,
- we're honest and open,
- we're one talented team,
- we strive for excellence.
- We lead, learn and inspire.

Each of which is then supported by a set of competencies that we use for recruitment, appraisal and all of those things, trying to embed that whole culture.

All that came from people so when we played it back to them there was a recognition 'Oh yes we see that. That's what we said!' That's how we made sure there's a connection between people's felt experience and what's coming back to them in terms of the South Manchester Way.

When we launched the South Manchester Way we launched it in such a way that was very interactive, a bit of a different way that people weren't quite as used to, you know lots of cutting out of paper and making figures and drawing and moving around. Standing in each other's footprints and telling stories and all those things kind of which take people outside their usual routines but make them think about themselves and about their colleagues and about how they work together and about the South Manchester Way and what it actually means.

We did a big launch event at Manchester Airport with all of the senior leaders including the consultants and then each of them went away to repeat the same things with their teams, leading ultimately to a kind of cascade of those activities. So that really was the start, it was framing the environment around the culture and the expectations. Then the important thing was about following that up and making sure that the South Manchester Way was common currency for everyone.

Then of course there's the challenge of 'Okay that's all well and good but how are we going to sort out the major problems we've got?' We were in a hole on performance. We were red-rated for governance with Monitor (we were in significant breach of our terms). So we had to deal with MRSA, A&E pressures and waiting times (seeing patients within 18 weeks). All three of those things were really important.

So we started the infection prevention campaign – Everyone's Responsibility – and we really tried to major on visible, a visible demonstration of it's everyone's responsibility. There was a big communications campaign which was in tune with the South Manchester Way and there were pictures of all the staff from cleaners to porters to heart surgeons bare below the elbow washing their hands, quotes saying 'This is really important.'

Some fun events like the Great Hospital Hand Wash where we got loads of kids and other people from the community to stand outside in the car park with all of our staff and washing their hands too . . . It was called Super Hands to the tune of Black Lace's 'Superman' do you know it? Clean your hands . . . and all that.

And then we did the now infamous YouTube video the Michael Jackson 'Beat It' [see http://www.youtube.com/watch?v=1iwFObIrpX8] which is now legendary in the organization. But that was great because it was a fun way of conveying a serious message.

That allied to a much more rigorous and robust performance management framework about knowing the board, knowing where every ward was in terms of its cleanliness, its hand washing, use of gel, all high impact interventions – all those things. I was looking at that on a monthly basis with Mandy, the Director of Nursing, and with the senior staff.

The whole executive team ran a series of roadshows and made sure every single member of staff attended a roadshow, say 100 staff at a time, where one of us would lead the roadshow and take them through the slide set of why infection prevention was a problem in the Trust and what we were doing about it and what they needed to do individually about it.

So that approach kind of galvanized everyone but more importantly it sort of set the tone for how we manage issues which was very much about engagement and communication supported by a strong performance management process. Not one which was shouting at people but much more using the information to investigate why things weren't working and where the outliers were. Giving people a sense of empowerment and engagement in the issue and understanding why it mattered.

And the results of that process were that we have reduced MRSA by about 70 per cent. We've got one of the lowest rates now in the north-west so that was great. That shows if you manage issues in the South Manchester Way in this kind of engaging with people it works, people get it and they respond to it.

Me: This was a very courageous move though, people tend to think 'Well we've got burning issues now and we need a solution now! I can't do the culture stuff because we've got this to do first.' So here, do you think you've proved that actually by taking a step back and doing the South Manchester Way that meant that you could progress?

Julian: Yes, yes definitely. And that, that's absolutely the case because you change the way that people respond and work together. Change their mindset about looking for solutions and just create a much more of a positive culture around this rather than a blame culture.

We're taking a similar approach to our big challenge at the moment which is financial savings given the major challenges the public sector faces. We've got what we call our Fit for 15 Programme which is 15% of cost out over the next three years and we have taken a similar approach with road shows. Everyone, staff understanding the problems, understanding the scale of the challenge and already staff suggestions alone have yielded £400,000 which we wouldn't have known about.

There are the big strategic schemes that we've got but there's also the bottom-up stuff where people come with ideas and suggestions because they see the need for that and can connect it to the part of South Manchester Way which is about using our resources effectively and so on and that's really encouraging.

What we try and do with every kind of problem is come at it from that perspective. We have done some tough stuff though we've taken out a tier of management because part of the message coming from people in that first round was we've got too many managers, it feels top heavy (decisions take a long time, there are tiers and layers of management) so we've gone with what we call a clinical leadership model where we've put a lot of the clinicians in management roles, made them far more accountable but given them more responsibility in order to bring them right into the kind of mainstream of running the organization.

Now they're not on the sidelines complaining about things or feeling that they're detached from things. That's starting to embed now but it has meant a change in philosophy of the way we're organized, with clinicians much more exposed to financial issues, performance issues as well as clinical ones.

Me: How's that worked then because there's that you know from an outsider's point of view people say 'Well, shouldn't the clinicians just be concentrating on what they do best?'

Julian: Yes

Me: 'And why share such a valuable expertise with something that is not their forte?'

Julian: Well they're not full-time managers. They spend around anywhere between 10 to 20 per cent of their time on management but these are senior clinicians, they're supported by a full-time business manager and the matron. They work as a team.

And because every clinician in this Trust every day makes decisions whether they know it or not about resources and commitment of resources, it's really important that they're connected to that process. We think that we've got the balance about right in that nine of our senior clinicians, our clinical directors spend 10 to 20 per cent of their time on management but the rest of the time they're still doctors. They're still seeing patients but the thing is they've got the knowledge and understanding of what's happening that they convey to their teams in their Directorates.

So there's a strong sense of they know what's going on whereas a lot of the feedback I had when I started was things get decided up there somewhere and we have no idea why or and it causes problems and we don't understand what's going on. So bringing them much closer to the action so that as an Exec Team we sit down every month with the clinical directors and work through those issues is vital. And that's starting to work well.

Me: You've talked about culture a lot. Company culture is dependent on the people that are within the organization and the environment that you give them to work within. So you've tried to change the environment you have given people to work within. So how do you think they've responded to that?

Julian: Generally really well, some sceptics. Some people saying, you'd hear it now and again when some people are under pressure and do something someone will say 'Oh that's not very South Manchester Way.' That's quite good because you get a sense that at least people are challenging each other.

We're still in transition in terms of the new clinical leadership model. We've put all the clinical leaders including the matrons and the business managers and the clinical directors altogether through a clinical leadership programme with Manchester Business School. So they're all getting development together.

There will still be that transition to work through but I think people understand the context, the culture, the framework that we're working in much better now but it's been quite challenging for some people, particularly some managers who preferred the certainties of the old methods (we're able to kick the backsides of people they needed to make things happen).

Whereas this is more demanding – actually I think it requires more skill and working through (influencing) and it's a different approach. We use the South Manchester Way in terms of competencies to recruit people to so that we can describe very clearly what it is we're after. And we use it in appraisal as well. And those things are important because if you keep that going eventually over time we'll get to a point where we've got a much fuller coverage of it through all staff. Sooner or later the people that aren't in tune with it will leave because it becomes the predominant culture. That's the thing about culture it's massively important in terms of how you feel about your work and you feel about the organization.

Trying to increase the sense of affiliation that people have with UHSM is important. So a lot of the recognition that we do, a lot of the external prizes and awards that we win is important to reinforce the sense of we're on the right track, this is working. The fact that we're now one of the best performing Trusts in Manchester. We're green-rated for governance not red-rated and we're now out of the woods with the Regulator, all of that validates the approach that we've taken. That this was the right thing to do and that we shouldn't be deflected from that method however difficult it gets.

Me: So in terms of a timeline how long did it take you to establish the South Manchester Way?

Julian: Well we launched it in December of last year so it took us about six months to develop and launch. Then implementation, you never stop. We've been at it a year and when I meet with groups of staff and say 'Have you heard of the South Manchester Way? What is it?' All the hands go up and people can describe it which is good.

Me: How many people roughly?

Julian: Everyone.

Me: Which is how many?

Julian: Oh 5,000, yes lots of people.

Me: So that's actually quite a short space of time to cover so many people.

Julian: Yes, yes. That like the infection prevention that kind of communication of a key message where you cascade it or you do a series of roadshows or you just get everyone in groups. You focus attention on that and have a real drive on it and the way we've tried to brand the organization and the messages and constant reinforcement of it is really important.

I think that the fact that I was new and we had some new members of the Board and the Exec Team helped us signal a change. Therefore we were able to move quite quickly with it and people were quite receptive to it because we'd already been through a process of enquiry and consultation and getting a sense of what people thought and then feeding back to them what they'd said and shaping that which worked really well.

And I think often what I do in any organization now in terms of any leadership role is just to find out where people are at. Understand what they think about the job, what they think about the organization. Just absorb all that and then make sense of it and then put it into some sort of structure that speaks to people's sense of what they want the organization to be. It's always the same, it's invariably the same as what you want to do because people are aspirational and want success and so you find that common ground and use that and don't over complicate it.

Me: In terms of hard business metrics was there pressure from the people that you answer to?

Julian: Yes.

Me: You were in quite a desperate situation so you had a number of things that had to come together at one time.

Julian: Yes that's right. I was under pressure from the Board to deliver, from Monitor the Regulator to deliver. We held our nerve by saying we're not going to sort the 18 week issue out, for another eight months. It's going to take us this time to do it and try to be really honest about how long it's going to take to fix the problem and stick to that. We set milestones along the way so that we could see that things were improving.

That was the approach we took, I got some staff who were interested in this approach to come to the Board and tell the Board what they told me about the organization. The Board heard it for themselves about people's experience of the organization and why it needed to change.

Then there was no doubt. It wasn't just me saying this it was people that were prepared to step up to the mark and that included secretaries, nurses, consultants you know a cross-section were able to tell the Board the truth about the organization. That gave me a very strong mandate to move and deliver on that, while at the same time obviously pushing on the hard metrics.

But you've got to do that, if you only push on the hard metrics all you do is just repeat that sense of hitting people harder and asking more and more from them without the kind of sense of what this is all about. What are we all here to do? MRSA matters because it kills patients and patient care is at the heart of all we do, because we've all said that, we've all agreed that. Beating MRSA is more than just a management target that must be met.

And people don't like being told 'you must do'. I think that when people can see it is the right thing to and that it follows a set of values that are important, then it makes sense to them.

Me: Is there something that you look back on and just think 'Oh my we should not have done that.'

Julian: Yes probably quite a few to be honest. We've had to balance the development of the South Manchester Way with driving the performance and improving the performance. Worrying about how quickly the performance was going to turn and putting our faith in this approach and thinking 'Can we . . . Is this going to work?' because actually things aren't getting any better.

And I remember really worrying about MRSA and the cases not going down fast enough and thinking 'Have we got this right? Should we not just be getting people in and disciplining them?' You know? And actually we just kept faith with it and it did turn. I think that that's been one of the learning points that it's tempting to go back to what we all know as managers in terms of really hardcore bang and blame performance management but it's not a sustainable solution to high performance in any organization.

So in tough times employee engagement is more important than ever. And thinking about that, all the small things that we do make a difference to people, for example in the bad weather last January we got people to and from work and organized taxis and so on, it really made a difference.

It's a great thing to see a sense of community and a tangible sense of success and turnaround in the organization from where we were. But there's still more to do.

Me: It's the nature of transformation isn't it?

Julian: Absolutely.

Section 3
The Story

SWAP SHOP OF IDEAS

Step 17

A human process

Business transformation can't be delivered without employee engagement. Employees are genuinely scared when they hear the words transformation or change, not because they resist it but because it usually means it will affect their lives and they want reassurance or confirmation of that as quickly as possible.

Usually you can't do that at this stage.

As we are in a perpetual state of change and transformation is an ongoing process, transformation needs a rebranding exercise of its own. This is worth investing in because you need to dampen the yo-yo effect that this news generates in the emotions of the people who work for you.

You need to tell a story. The story of your business: where it started, the progress that has been made, the obstacles it faces, the opportunities it strives to capitalize on and how it's going to do that.

Everyone loves a story. Good storytellers use emotion and get us to believe in the characters in a way that helps us form a bond with them. It is far more compelling than giving people dry facts.

If you can involve your workforce in the story all the better; make it personal because it is to the people who work for you. People are emotional and they have more to worry about than what is happening at work.

If you treat each person like the individual they are, when you go through transformation you will have the full weight of that human capital behind your initiatives. If you avoid it or believe that it's not that important you will waste energy trying to convince people to be involved or not to jump ship too soon while trying to move through transformation.

If you are at the top of the organization it starts with you and works down. Don't think your managers don't need this kind of attention too. You give it to them and they pass it on.

Which do you think is the easier ride?

Take part in the discussion at www.cheeky-monkey.co/connect

Cheeky Monkey Wisdom

I love to know why people come to work and do what they do. It tells you so much about why they are there and what their motivation is. Some people live very complicated lives outside work having to juggle a number of things. If you understand that, you will know what they need to hear and how about your business transformation. Having lots of employees is no excuse for not doing this. The person at the top may struggle to remember everything but that's why there is a management team. Not knowing the people who work for you and how you should communicate to get the best out of them is just lazy.

Step 18

Getting others to see the light

Thankfully leading through dictatorship has more or less had its day. Even if you are the boss you need to get people on side and if you are lower down the food chain unless you can sell your vision then it won't see the light of day.

The difference between a good and a great sales person is PASSION. The kind of passion that shows your heart and soul are connected to the cause.

You have your map, the product of the first two sections of the book. It's not a proposal or plan yet: we are just trying to picture the end before we start. It's time to get the views of other people, the people who see and know more than you. You need to treat these people with respect because they are giving you something that is priceless, the chance to think outside your own head. Every piece of feedback has a value even if you choose to discount it later.

See this as a sales pitch: you want people to be as passionate about transformation as you are and you want them to give it some priority in their already jam-packed world. Even if you are the boss and could just turn round and say this is what we are doing, business transformation without employee engagement is not as successful as with it.

You are looking for buy-in and input.

Be honest about the things you don't know upfront; don't leave it for people to use the gaps as an opportunity to throw doubt at what you are saying. You know what you do know (the map). This is what you don't know yet:

- ▶ if everyone agrees with the map
- ▶ how many projects it will take to deliver the transformation

- ▸ the resources required to deliver them (people and money)
- ▸ tangible benefits
- ▸ the timeline.

That's where you need input. This is most effective done in a workshop environment where there is a process of storytelling, information exchange and collaborative input. Be clear about what you want to achieve upfront, get their attention and drive creativity.

Take part in the discussion at www.cheeky-monkey.co/connect

Cheeky Monkey Wisdom

Sales people used to be a different breed. Now thanks to eBay (and originally car boot sales) normal people sell all the time. Be bold, confident and self-assured. If you're not, they won't be. Be honest at all times: people smell a rat quickly and even if it's not intentional, it will make people wonder what is really going on. It is always better to say you don't know if you don't know. Don't try and be too clever.

Step 19

Disagree

Conflict is so important for a healthy business. It ensures that you are looking at all the options and have people who are passionate about their beliefs and willing to fight for what is right. This leaves you with well-thought-through arguments that can be analysed against what you are trying to achieve.

Some people avoid conflict because it's uncomfortable and can be personal. People can get defensive and there is always the fear that it might affect the relationship you have with people at work.

So, you may have to instigate conflict and show people that it's acceptable and will be rewarded.

- Let everyone know that their opinion is wanted and debate around those opinions and the ideas that follow is expected.
- Ask people their opinions first and look to engage people in disagreement so they know it's safe and acceptable.
- Praise the people who do it.
- Take the disagreement to a positive end showing how the conflict provided a needed challenge.
- Make sure your behaviour isn't putting people off.
- Encourage people to support their opinions with data.
- Don't allow personal attacks.

Disagreements and problem-solving go hand in hand – get stuck in.

Take part in the discussion at www.cheeky-monkey.co/connect

Cheeky Monkey Wisdom

When you instigate conflict, keep the sessions light-hearted. If your team haven't been encouraged to do this before, it will take them some time to get into the swing of it. Be aware that you can go from one extreme (polite nodding and general agreement) to the other (personal attacks stemmed from pent-up frustration); make sure you play referee. You are aiming for constructive debate not bloodshed and door slamming.

Step 20

....

Definitions: transformation vs. programmes vs. projects

I have already said that business transformation itself is not a project but projects do deliver the change required. If you have several projects that are aligned, you have a programme.

Keeping this simple, it's all about levels and managing dependencies so that lots of changes can happen at the same time without bringing your business to a grinding halt.

Programmes are focused on an overall outcome, usually to improve an organization's performance, and contain several related projects.

Projects deliver discrete chunks of change. Projects have a defined scope (beginning and end) and resources allocated to it (people, time and money). When a project gets done, something new exists that didn't exist before.

The business transformation timeline needs to be divided into discrete projects to deliver the change.

It will look like one continuous project because of the relationships we have made between what you have now and what you are trying to achieve, so we have to examine the deliverables. Turn this into a black and white situation: what are the ultimate deliverables that make the complete transformation successful?

- ▶ money?
- ▶ new products?
- ▶ building something?
- ▶ moving somewhere?
- ▶ buying something?
- ▶ implementing something new (equipment, IT or software)?
- ▶ new process?

- ▶ new ways of working?
- ▶ new skill sets?
- ▶ new people?

Once you have your list of ultimate deliverables, draw the links to the subcomponents that have to be delivered to get to the ultimate prize. I will give you a couple of Cheeky Monkey examples to help your thinking and understanding.

Cheeky Monkey Wisdom

Don't put structure and hierarchy into your transformation for the sake of it or worse to satisfy someone else's craving for status. The beauty of working in this environment is that the rules are just there to guide you. You are delivering change which means to a large extent you can dictate how that is best delivered.

Good project managers conduct the orchestra and are constantly projecting forward, measuring the risks and dealing with the impact of the issues in tireless pursuit of the ultimate prize. They are not co-ordinators or post boxes.

Cheeky Monkey Example 1

Deliver £3m profit by relocating the manufacturing of soap from the UK, Australia and Indonesia to a purpose-built factory in Thailand.

Ultimate prize = money

Sub-deliverables = build new factory, close UK factory, relocate production lines, recruit and train new employees, standardize product and pack format, optimize new supply chain.

Surely that was a programme of related projects? Yes, but in this case the project manager had to be able to play some tunes with what was going on to ensure that the ultimate goal was delivered. It was more efficient to have a strong project manager report directly into a steering group to keep decision-making fast and effective.

In this project, the ultimate prize was money and there were so many factors that influenced the financial forecast, some of which we could control (e.g. production-line-run rates, standardization of product and pack format) and some we could not (e.g. the price of raw materials, dropping sales volumes in the UK, shipping costs, employee costs – for the right people anyway). Each sub-deliverable had a delivery stream manager who managed the day-to-day reporting directly to the project manager

The project delivered 12 months early and £4m profit.

Cheeky Monkey Example 2

Deliver an Innovation Centre that will bring together three key components of the product development process: R&D, perfumery and manufacturing. Create a working environment that not only technically allows for industry-leading work to be produced but is inspirational and serves as a theatre to involve suppliers, customers and consumers.

Ultimate prize = a centre that will deliver next generation products through collaboration

Sub-deliverables = a factory, a laboratory, a perfumery, a collaborative working space, new ways of working, new policies and a return on investment schedule.

This one was a programme of related projects. Although everything still had to come together and money was still a deliverable, the environment was more stable and we could influence and control the large elements of change (new build through contracts) and the pace of change could be structured and monitored more effectively through project managers reporting into a programme manager and steering group.

The Innovation Centre opened on target and was the start of a fundamental shift in policy and ways of working for the group. Subsequent projects have followed the same format.

Take part in the discussion at www.cheeky-monkey.co/connect

Cheeky Monkey Wisdom

There can be a power struggle between project managers and programme managers because the reporting line should not really be hierarchical. Both roles should present to the steering group but there are often times when that results in conflict, which you should see as a good thing but you need to consider how you resolve the conflict carefully (leaving them to it, which of course would be preferred is not ideal and can result in fighting in the playground). Take the roles back to basics: the programme manager looks to achieve the overall outcome and so spends most of their time projecting forward and thinking about the 'what ifs'. The project manager is focused on their bit, the issues they have delivering their bit in the here and now. Always focus on the greater good – short-term gain usually brings long-term pain.

Step 21

Design the results

Once you chunk up your deliverables into programmes and projects, you get a chance to design your results before you start. It's a practice run to see if you are happy with what you are going to get and be clear about where it is coming from (see Step 23 – The reward).

Your business deliverables and the priority that you have given them need to be your focus here. There is always a trade-off between putting the fire out and delivering change that will not only put the fire out but stop it restarting again. Of course the latter takes longer but the rewards are sustainable. If you have several things that need doing then you have the opportunity to mix things up and schedule some short-term fixes (remove frustrations and blockers) alongside some more sustainable fixes.

No one wants to work on projects that take years before they deliver any benefit anymore and finance directors definitely don't want to sign them off. The project may be the same; it ultimately takes the same time before it is completed but the skill is in how you design the delivery of results along that timeline.

Take part in the discussion at www.cheeky-monkey.co/connect

The way we work with clients has changed dramatically. It was usual to get a project that would run over one, two, three years and the focus was on the end goal. Now we get opportunities to work on several projects with a shorter horizon and in demand is the skill to design the results and manoeuvre resources and priorities. More projects, done better, delivered faster.

Step 22

....

Money and people

You will need both. You have your timeline with a programme and projects chunked up to show what needs to be delivered as part of the transformation process. Even with our futuristic eyes that are focused on the end, without planning backwards in some detail we don't really know. So guess; that's all an estimate is. Think about where you are today and where you are trying to go: use your experience with confidence.

And of course there is the difference between need and want. Establish both.

Take part in the discussion at www.cheeky-monkey.co/connect

Cheeky Monkey Wisdom

Don't be defeatist with this. Fight the voices in your mind that are saying you have no idea or that the guess won't stand up to challenge. If you know that, you know what the challenge is going to be and you are already one step ahead.

Establishing need and want gives you negotiating room and a baseline. Remember this is not about you – don't be tempted to be a hero! Ego at this stage only serves to give you more work when the project starts.

62

Step 23

The reward

Not all transformation projects deliver money to the bottom line but it is a constant ask so you need to know what you want and need to get out of doing this. Lots of business transformation projects include the implementation of IT and/or software. IT usually enables the transformation but in itself rarely delivers bottom-line benefit. If money is your driver for business transformation then you have to be clear about where it is coming from.

If money is not your driver then you have to be clear what is. Money does make the world go round and it is amazing how many times it ends up being the focus of transformation review meetings when it was happily accepted as not being the driver upfront.

The reward has to align to the business deliverables.

Take part in the discussion at www.cheeky-monkey.co/connect

Cheeky Monkey Wisdom

All roads on the business transformation journey lead to money but they are not always in your project. Who gets to claim the reward can be a contentious issue. Being clear about this now will also help to decide if this transformation is really a project or just part of business as usual.

Step 24

Action

Action makes all the difference. Don't over-analyse. You do not know everything and that is the perfect place to start. If you knew everything you would be at the end. What you do have is a concise and well-thought-through scope signed up to by the decision-makers who can picture what success looks like.

Not every business needs a business plan to be successful. But when you are delivering business transformation you need a business transformation plan for the transformation to be successful if you want to see your business transformed within a specified timeframe, within a predetermined budget, delivering something tangible.

Planning is action.

What timeline is this transformation going to be delivered in? We could be talking about anything from the introduction of a new way of working to the implementation of an integrated IT-enabled business architecture and everything in between. You need to help me here, figure out when it needs to be done by to capture all the opportunities, add in known timeframes for work that has to be done by an external supplier and work backwards. If that means you had to start in 2010 or earlier you have a problem!

Timelines are subject to resource. Generally if you can throw resource at it then you can have it quicker (not always but generally). Resource costs money – at this stage it's all about the maths.

Take part in the discussion at www.cheeky-monkey.co/connect

Cheeky Monkey Wisdom

People hate planning. Of course there are people whose jobs it is to plan; they are the exception to the rule. It is a necessary evil and so ignore the pained cries of 'it will be out of date straight away', 'we are only guessing at this stage', 'how do we know what's going to happen?', 'we will only have to change it' – all valid but don't let this stop you. The plan is your baseline: with these assumptions, if nothing changes, this is what is going to happen.

Step 25

Choices, decisions and consequences

We are all really enthusiastic about change. Gone are the days of resistance in the way it existed in the 2000s. We jump on new initiatives like it's an escape from our real job. Resistance to change now comes from two simple areas that are best tackled upfront, head on and with integrity and honesty:

- ▶ Do I get to keep my job? (the affect on our lives outside of work)
- ▶ Are we in this together or is this being done to me? (How much control and influence do I have?)

There are always choices, which means that there are always decisions to be made and as a result of those choices and decisions there are ultimately consequences. Being weak in this area helps nobody. We live in a world where people face harsh choices and decisions, and the consequences of those every day. Yet when people come to work we think they need to be protected.

Even at this stage of looking at the end and scoping backwards there will be some choices and decisions that are genuinely so clear they are going to happen. Others you will not know. If you are responsible for making those choices then now is the time to be straight and tell it like it is because backtracking is always messy.

Where there are choices, there are decisions.

Take part in the discussion at www.cheeky-monkey.co/connect

Cheeky Monkey Wisdom

Remember we are picturing the end and working backwards to create an outline of what this business transformation is going to do, with what and why. We have our best guess on the table. This makes people very nervous, they usually want data to support decisions (back-covering) – do not use this as an excuse to shirk making choices and decisions! You know what you need to do and there is risk associated with it – you will manage the risk and make changes as the situation requires.

STORY 3: IT'S GOT TO BE FUN!

Storyteller: Martin Davies, CEO, Holidaybreak PLC

In 1994 Martin founded Tommy Boy Music in Europe. Martin established Tommy Boy Music as one of Europe's top independent record labels setting up offices in London and Hamburg and distribution partnerships in every major market across the continent. In 1997 Martin moved to New York becoming president of parent company Tommy Boy Inc., helping to establish the company as an iconic independent music brand. In 2003 Tommy Boy Music was sold to Time-Warner.

He joined PGL as Chief Executive in 2004 and went on to lead the management buy-out in 2005. PGL is a market-leading provider of activity courses and holidays – whether for schools, for whom they provide educational tours, adventure courses and skiing trips or for youth groups – family holidays and summer camps for unaccompanied children.

He subsequently led the sale of PGL to Holidaybreak in June 2007, following which he was appointed Managing Director of the Education Division and became a member of the PLC Board. Martin became Group Chief Executive in 2010 and also retained the role of Managing Director of the Education Division in addition to his new duties.

Me: Martin, you have the Midas touch when it comes to business transformation, first Tommy Boy Europe, then Tommy Boy Inc., PGL, now Holidaybreak Group – do you think you could transfer these skills to transform any business?

Martin: No. I am best working with a business that has an emotional attachment with its customer.

When you've got a business that really does care for the customer, particularly on an emotional scale, you can do things in that business you can't with others. What I try to do, whether at Tommy Boy or at PGL, is first of all understand, what is that relationship.

The more complex a product becomes and the more things you're doing for your customers that are hard to replicate, the more I get excited because that, to me, means you can build a relationship not just with your product and customer but the people working in your business.

Me: What makes a great business?

Martin: A business that focuses on the customer, where at every stage there is an element of proper respect for the people that you deal with. You're not just there to make money. It has to be way more than just that or where there is that priority (this was a big driving force at Tommy Boy), you learned from your customer, you can't sit back from them, you have to actually work on their side, so that your customer is part of your business if you like. That it always has to be fun. If it's not fun it's not worth doing, for me, I don't see the point in it.

Doing things is better than talking about doing things. For so many people it's 'This is what we're about to do,' rather than, 'This is what we did.' They can always articulate far more clearly what they're about to do. I try to say, 'tell me what you've done,' and then it's more revealing.

I find that in most businesses that work, they'll tell you what they're doing, what they've done and what they're about to do but in the same sentence, it's all progressive.

At Tommy Boy, the mantra we had was 'Have fun. Do good. Make money.' That was how we started off … we're doing it because we liked what we're doing.

So, we tried to think, 'How do you make money out of that without spoiling it?' There has to be an element of more than to get rich. The real reason is your relationship between your product and your customer. Having fun is nearly always the way that engages all those things together.

It's what we've done at Holidaybreak, linking all the things into business objectives.

Me: At what point does something stop being real and start being contrived?

Martin: At the point at which you're doing it to serve your business rather than your customer. Our customer doesn't have to conform to us; we have to conform to the customer.

People can come up with business plans that actually don't excite customers, don't excite anyone. You have to find out what the customers want and keep focused.

You're not there to honour the economics. Don't get attached to things, get rid of them if they're not working and don't worry about it. Even if you've spent a lot of money on an IT system, if it's not serving the customer throw it away because it's going to kill your business.

We get rid of investments as quickly as we take advantage of them because they're in the way of your business growing.

Me: From a business planning perspective then, how structured is your planning process and how rigidly do you follow it?

Martin: Well, it can be structured in a business like PGL because we can actually sell things to customers so far ahead of us delivering them that it makes planning incredibly tangible. We can do nutty things and if they don't work, if customers don't buy them, we don't deliver them.

We've got a brilliant business model. We don't have to worry about NPD [new product development], we can innovate with our customers.

In the music business, the whole idea of the business plan was nuts because that was a series of things that would be nice if they happened. It would be nice if De La Soul delivered their next album within a 12-month period that you're forecasting for but they might not. It would be nice if it was as successful as the multi-platinum album we had the year before but it might not.

You might plan for a year where you haven't got any artists that you know the reasonable demand levels for and you get a new artist and the sales go nuts. So, effectively the idea of what you're prepared to invest in your product development is far more important than what you're going to gain from the other side.

You have to be prepared that in one or two years you're going to actually make less money and other years you're going to make a hell of a lot of money.

Me: So, you constantly put the customer at the centre of the transformation?

Martin: They have to be.

Me: So much so they dictate what you do?

To an extent, in the music less so (apart from absolutely extreme tastemakers) most people are unaware what they want until they're given it. If you're about cutting-edge music you really do have to make sure that you're innovating but you innovate by understanding.

You don't suddenly impose something on them, you actually work alongside them. You're an extension of the lifestyle, an extension of things that are currently relevant to them. So, you have to understand them even more if you're innovating.

Me: Your new challenge is to transform Holidaybreak, how's that going?

Martin: My challenge at Holidaybreak really has been to make it feel like a business where everyone's a stakeholder in the product because they're emotionally attached to it.

Me: You started with PGL, how did that go?

Martin: Yes, we bought PGL, developed it, and changed it radically but we kept the product and the customer faithful to the original promise. There was a great product there in the first place. We just improved it but we didn't lose one member of staff while we grew over 100 per cent. Every single person that was here when I came is still here.

They're all here because we've kept that big relationship between the love they have for the product and they love they have for what they do.

Me: I remember when we first came; one of the things that you said to us was that the working environment had to feel like what it is we do.

Martin: Yes.

Me: We provide holidays for kids.

Martin: No, we provide challenges for kids.

Me: Oops, of course!

Martin: It is easier to provide a child with a holiday! To do what we do at PGL, you have to understand the child's needs and help them to unravel their potential. It's more satisfying to do the things that we do for them because they're more three-dimensional. I mean anyone could come in and do what we do, if it was just holidays. It's more complicated than that and therefore harder to replicate.

Me: You have then tried to replicate that in a much bigger group now?

Martin: First of all replicated it by making PGL much bigger.

Me: Sounds so simple, was it?

Martin: Well yes, PGL was a business that made £850,000 in 2003/4 and I think it made slightly less than £14 million last year. So, that has completely transformed.

Me: Is the definition of success the financial results?

Martin: I don't want to say we succeeded because we made so much money, but that is one of the calibrations of success. But they way we achieved our growth was by being faithful to the core values we have as a business and not compromising on that.

That is really hard to measure but confirmation to me that we are doing it right came at our company lunch in December (we call it lunch rather than a company conference). Despite the fact that we were reviewing a business that is now transformed, the spirit, the fun, the socializing during the afternoon, the self-deprecating speeches that our staff made worked the same way as it did when we made £850k. That's, to me, that's the success of transformation, sustainability.

Section 4
Doing It and Delivering It

Step 26

The environment

Delivering the components that make up the business transformation
you want to see is at least as important as the business that you are
running day to day and needs to be treated that way. Projects are so
often given to people to do in addition to their day job. I'm not saying
this is automatically bad, they might be the right people and they
may have the space to do this job on top of their own but you need to
know that.

Programme and project management is a skill set and discipline
like any other function in the business; the way you treat the people
delivering and the space they have to work in will shape their view on
how important this is and the priority and energy they should give it.

Physical space to be able to work, hold meetings and create an
welcoming environment for team members to drop round when they
have issues or concerns is brilliant. Wall space to put up timelines and
progress updates is great. Electronic space to be able to file project
documents in a shared area is becoming increasingly important.

Creating programmes and projects electronically is the way forward,
creating an area where all project documents can be linked to the
timeline and tasks detailed in work flow that makes it clear who has to
deliver what and by when, all net-based to allow for virtual working.

The environment must satisfy the need for:

▶ time
▶ skill set
▶ physical working
▶ electronic space.

Take part in the discussion at www.cheeky-monkey.co/connect

74

Cheeky Monkey Wisdom

Leading a transformation programme or project is an honour. You have the opportunity to shape the new direction that the business is going to take, it's new, and it needs care and an energy source that is going to be able to navigate the ups and downs with ease. You can't do it without your team and they can make life really hard or really enjoyable. It is rare that project teams are dedicated to one project; your team members will have loads of conflicting priorities so making them feel connected to your project is important. You need to use your physical and electronic space to do that. Project names, branding, shared documents, progress updates, risks and issues should be visible so that people can identify with what is going on quickly and easily.

Step 27

Over-communicate

We have our map, programme (maybe) and projects (at least one, probably more), key stakeholders have bought in. We are ready to tell everyone everything but you shouldn't! This is not about being open and transparent, this is about understanding the need to generate two-way communications and to have a communication plan that assumes people will engage. You want to hear that engagement, you will not just talk to them. Consider:

1 You have something to communicate: the story – scope of the business transformation, the background (SWOT), the current challenges, the gaps, the picture of the future and the choices that have already been made on what's in and out, the reasons why and an overall timeline for the transformation process to be realized. This should be communicated to EVERYBODY.

2 Communication is a two-way process. You want to receive feedback; the ability to listen is one of the most important management skills you can develop.

3 People like to process and react to information in different ways and you want their involvement to be genuine and thought through. You communicate first, take questions and follow up with workshops when the information has been digested and some proper engagement can start.

4 Towards the end of the communication session you can tell everyone about the workshops and those who may be getting involved. Don't act like it is a done deal and you are just there to tell them what they are doing. They have a choice (they may not really but you want them to believe that they do). This process of engagement will underpin the framework of your transformation – we are going to transform this business.

5 At the end tell everyone how they will hear regular updates – intranet, notice boards, briefings, newsletter, etc. – and the next time you (or someone else) will talk to them. Go for an inspirational big finish, a recap on the picture that everyone is working towards and why it's great.

Take part in the discussion at www.cheeky-monkey.co/connect

Cheeky Monkey Wisdom

The majority of people who work for you want to be involved and do the best that they can do to contribute to the success of the business. There are some who are just sheep – they want an easy life and are happy to follow the majority. And then there are those who are just damaged, have been through stuff that has made them cynical and unable to trust (thankfully only a small number but it might sound like there is more). Don't let the sheep be captured by the damaged.

Step 28

Create involvement

What is said in the communication session is not a one-off thing; you have to mean it because it has to be maintained from the moment you leave the room. The management team needs to know that if someone wants to discuss it they must find time, they don't leave the room and go back to business as usual until the next project review. Business transformation is a management initiative that is now firmly part of your business. How you listen and respond to feedback will either feed the naysayers or the people who want it to work; the sheep will be watching carefully.

Perception is reality.

Take part in the discussion at www.cheeky-monkey.co/connect

Cheeky Monkey Wisdom

Keep to the facts. It's early days and there is so much you don't know. Don't get carried away with the storytelling. People have long memories.

Step 29

Establish authority

This has to happen up and down the organization (remember the key drivers in Step 1). You need to create knowledge through your business and nurture the scarce human capital that will get the job done. All these plans don't get the job done; the people do.

Employee empowerment is an overused empty term in lots of places; make it mean something in yours. Basics for leaders:

▶ Take your work seriously but not yourself. Make yourself accessible and available.
▶ Be decisive over the tough stuff.
▶ Don't wait for all the facts to make a decision, go with your instincts.
▶ Simplify things so everyone can understand. Don't hide behind numbers or data, show how you use them with your own judgement.
▶ Be forever the optimist.
▶ Know that the devil is always in the detail. Delve beneath the surface all the time.
▶ Challenge everything.
▶ Don't tell people what they have done is great if it isn't. People need to value a pat on the back.
▶ Show that job titles are meaningless and give opportunities as rewards to people who show integrity, energy, balance and drive.
▶ Reward delivery of change (even really small things) instead of general performance.

Basics for employees:

▶ See what you can get away with.
▶ Don't constantly ask for approval.

- See what your leaders are doing and go for it.
- 'Be the change you want to see.' (Gandhi)

Take part in the discussion at www.cheeky-monkey.co/connect

Cheeky Monkey Wisdom

People are generally sceptical of this approach and the realities of establishing authority through the organization as opposed to top-down. They need coaching, gentle nudges that it is okay and encouragement to take the lead. This is really worth the investment as you will see people blossom before your eyes. The way the management team behave is of course essential to the success of this. In my experience the middle management layer struggles and becomes a barrier to change if not nurtured and coached in the same way.

Step 30

The project kick-off

This is individual to each project: each project must have its own and they need to last at least a day. You give the project team the scope and they turn that into a document that represents their promise, what they believe they need to do to deliver that scope and their commitment to each other on how it's going to be done.

The project manager should lead this session and it should be mandatory that all of the project team members attend. This is a key part of the employee empowerment process and they need to be encouraged to do the following:

- ▶ Challenge the scope. Do this team think it's correct? Will it deliver what is required?
- ▶ Break the scope down into objectives. This is how this team thinks it can deliver what is being asked. Objectives must be SMART (Specific, Measurable, Attainable, Realistic and Time-bound).
- ▶ Break the objectives down into discrete work packages that can be assigned to individuals for delivery.
- ▶ Take the financial headlines and create a budget you are comfortable you can work within.
- ▶ Look at the dependencies between the work that needs to be delivered and link them.
- ▶ Agree a timeline and ensure that everyone knows who is responsible and accountable for delivery.
- ▶ Agree what is critical to the project and when the team would say the project was in distress.
- ▶ Brainstorm all the things that might happen to derail the project (risks). Make sure someone is responsible for managing them.
- ▶ Identify all of the things that are already happening that need resolving to keep the project on track. Assign them as actions.

- Sign up to a progress reporting process and updates.
- Sign up to the fact you can deliver or go back to the steering group with the reasons why you think you can't and discuss alternative options.

Take part in the discussion at www.cheeky-monkey.co/connect

Cheeky Monkey Wisdom

The project kick-off is such an important session because it marks:

- The transfer of ownership of the project to the project manager and project team.
- The opportunity for the project manager to establish authority and ways of working in the project.
- The team's decision on whether they can deliver what has been asked of them and return to base with options if they think they can't.
- The team's decision on how they deliver what has been asked of them.

How the steering group behaves when the team returns to them will dictate the level of belief in the empowerment they have been given.

Step 31

The steering group

The steering group isn't a powerhouse of executives who want to carry the senior status of being involved with the project. There are specific roles and responsibilities that enable this group to be effective, supportive and well-balanced in the decisions they have to take during the life of the project, namely:

▶ **Sponsor.** The person who has everything to gain from this project delivering. They write (or they might tell you what to write) and own the business case. They get the deciding vote on what gets done, should that point arise, and they are senior enough to kick some butt should the whole thing start losing momentum and/or direction.

▶ **Senior user.** This is the most senior person you have who can represent the users who have to live with what the project is delivering when it becomes business as usual (the clue is in the title). This person makes sure the needs of those who will use the final product are paramount and bats for them at all times during the project. You may have more than one senior user, especially if it's a global change or a significant change affecting more than one area of the business.

▶ **Senior supplier.** This is the most senior person you have who can represent those designing, developing, facilitating, procuring, implementing, and possibly operating and maintaining the project's deliverables. This person makes sure that any conflicts between what the users want and what the suppliers are giving them are balanced and worked through, maintaining the quality of the project deliverables.

▶ **Project director/manager.** Depending on the size of the project you may have two separate roles of project director and project manager, with the project director providing more ongoing support to the project manager outside steering group sessions. If your project isn't big enough, the roles can be combined. The project manager has the authority to run the project on a day-to-day basis on behalf of the steering group within the constraints laid down by them and agreed in the project definition document. The project manager is there to make sure the project delivers what is expected within time and budget. If there are problems, they flag them quickly with options (impact to deliverables assessed) for the steering group to agree action on.

Motivating and keeping the energy in the team up and focused on delivery, while having the foresight to see and deal with the impact of change without derailing the project, is their core role.

Take part in the discussion at www.cheeky-monkey.co/connect

Cheeky Monkey Wisdom

Presenting to the steering group might be the first time that some of these project managers or team members have had to communicate with senior managers in the business. It can be intimidating and your status within the business will follow through into the steering group if you let it – try not to let that happen. You don't want a situation where more time is spent prepping for the steering group than is spent on tangible project deliverables. Make it clear what you want to see and the format you want to see it in. Your role is to challenge but not dismiss. If the project team put issues on the table, ask for solutions but don't ignore them. You need to foster an environment of openness and trust or the team won't tell you things are wrong until it's too late.

Step 32

Beyond the sexy start

Maintenance is boring. Business transformation is as much about maintenance as it is making sure the sexy start goes well and, depending on your personality type, one will probably be harder than the other. Keeping things going is about discipline and belief.

Once the project starts, you have to contend with it and the general running of the business and there are constant conflicts of time. The project can't come second. Business transformation is part of the running of your business, so this has to be about being disciplined about what you do and how you do it.

Steering group meetings should be scheduled ahead, with at least one a month. The project team need to work to the schedule and changing the dates helps no one. Make life easy so people can contribute. Not everyone will be able to make every meeting but they can always contribute. Ensure information is circulated prior to the meeting and read it. Remember the devil is in the detail and you must look beneath the surface.

Don't wait for meetings to see how things are going. Make time to drop in on the project manager and team and get a casual update. Look at the information on the project system, particularly the risks and issues logs. Talk about the project so people know you are looking. This isn't about Big Brother watching, this is about setting an example that, despite things being busy, everything gets the attention it needs.

If your enthusiasm for these things drops as time goes on, so will that of others working on the project.

Should the tables be reversed and you see your project managers and/ or teams starting to ignore the discipline of new ways of working then you need to check what is happening.

- Have they got too much to do? If so, encourage them to come forward with solutions to the resource problem.
- Are they just trying to short-cut the process? If so, there will be consequences.

Take part in the discussion at www.cheeky-monkey.co/connect

Cheeky Monkey Wisdom

This is where it's important to make sure the load has been spread and everyone is empowered. Being the go-to person is relentless when business transformation is in play. People who try and be the hero and be all things to all people always end up failing. You are aiming for sustainable change in a business that is transformed by all the people in it, who understand responsibility, accountability and consequences. Consequences do not equal blame culture; don't be scared of pulling up someone who is working against the change – it can do wonders for the rest of the team.

Step 33

Breaking the habit

It is no secret that habits are hard to break; the clever people at MIT discovered our brain has a habit section where it stores information that we perceive to be important. The messages in there can be changed but they have a memory, so when you see or do something that is familiar to that habit, the memory comes back and so does the urge to do it.

A lot of what happens in business transformation is about breaking habits. We have to recognize that it is a journey and sometimes we just return to old habits. Recognizing this and doing something about it is where a change in behaviour is required. Don't confuse the signs of withdrawal with the sense that things are not working; it's at this dip in the journey that everything seems hard work. People may jump on the opportunity to derail, and politics and opposition may try and take over.

Take part in the discussion at www.cheeky-monkey.co/connect

Cheeky Monkey Wisdom

See this stage in the journey for what it is, breaking of habits and changing behaviour. You can't ignore it but you can tackle the issues and barriers head on and move through them. Some people will decide they don't want to change their behaviour – that's up to them – but there will be consequences if that derails what you are trying to do as a business. This needs to be dealt with as adults. Behaviour is a business performance measure, and if there is no longer a match between what the individual wants and what the business wants there is only one conclusion to be drawn.

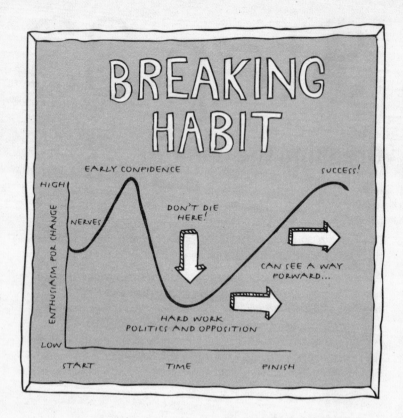

Step 34

Garbage in, garbage out

Garbage in, garbage out is computing slang for 'if you input the wrong data, the results will also be wrong.' The term came from the programming community, where instructors remind students that they must check and re-check their data and coding to ensure that the results are valid, as computers will happily process wrong information and return a result.

This is now valid everywhere for all of us. We can make our processes and use of system so automated that people forget they are the intelligence in this equation and under times of pressure and stress they get lazy or worse, thinking no one will check. Guess what? Most of the time they don't.

Your business transformation will result in data and information flowing, particularly numbers, and you and others will make critical decisions based on these. You have to check the logic, the way they have been put together and the assumptions that have been made. This doesn't mean that you are doing the job again, just by doing those three things errors usually jump off the page.

This kind of diligence makes a real difference to how your teams do the work in the first place and, if it doesn't, you have different decisions to make.

Take part in the discussion at www.cheeky-monkey.co/connect

Cheeky Monkey Wisdom

Attention to detail and looking around a problem are skills that require practice and discipline. People generally want to do a good job but they naturally see what is deemed to be acceptable. If you accept garbage, more will be produced. If you don't and you are clear about what is acceptable, you will get what is acceptable. We are simple creatures really.

Step 35

Value what you do

As you go through this journey of business transformation, despite your best efforts at planning, not everything will be clear and there will be ambiguity for people to deal with. At these times people are happier if they can align what's going on with what they value and believe in, and there should be a link from that to what the business values and believes in.

For your empowered employees to feel confident in making decisions when all is not certain, they need to know that what they value and believe in is true, and matches what the business values and believes in.

At the start of business transformation you will have shared those values and beliefs as part of the Story; it will have been uplifting and inspirational. When you are into the doing and delivering the message, things may seem blurred. People who are going through the process of breaking habits and behavioural change may question if this is still something they value or believe in and whether anyone in the business really cares.

Take time to give updates that show how the business is transforming through the change that people are working on and how that is underpinned by the business values and beliefs.

Take part in the discussion at www.cheeky-monkey.co/connect

Cheeky Monkey Wisdom

Don't be one of those businesses that spends money on creating mission and values, communicates them, laminates them and puts them up on boards around the place and on each person's desk or security pass and then does nothing with them again. It makes people cynical.

Step 36

Shortcuts can be good

Business transformation is a journey and when you are on it you will discover things and meet people who can help. Be open to that all the time because these are potential shortcuts for you.

You don't have to reinvent the wheel or make life harder than it needs to be so that you experience the pain of doing everything: if you get to the end goal without some of the pain – brilliant!

Learning all you can from the resources available to you and investing in the right mentors, the right education and the right products is like taking a shortcut. You will save time and make more money by learning from those who already have the information and experience you're looking for.

Take part in the discussion at www.cheeky-monkey.co/connect

Cheeky Monkey Wisdom

Being a consultant has a stigma attached to it and if we can avoid using the term we do. In my employed career I watched many consultants join us, suck up the knowledge we had, go and tell our bosses what we had been saying for ages, get listened to and walk away with a fat cheque leaving us to do the work. Obviously that is rubbish and doesn't help anyone. Don't let those experiences stop you getting help in a way that helps you achieve your goals in a sustainable way. The drivers in Step 1 create a new workforce, happy to work with you, but not necessarily for you. They have a wealth of experience and a work ethic that is very valuable during business transformation and will add value to your journey.

Step 37

....

Things that might stop you

Things that might stop you, that may or may not happen, are risks. They need managing and should be captured at different levels in the business transformation process:

- ▶ They are input at the grassroots level through projects.
- ▶ Project managers escalate them to the steering group.
- ▶ Programme managers report risks against the overall outcome.
- ▶ The steering group align back to business goals.
- ▶ Ultimately they will be managed by the leadership team.

The process of risk management creates value because it is part of the decision-making process. Obviously risks may or may not happen, so you will only have the information available at the time. Because of that, structure is required in the collection and assessment of any possible risk:

- ▶ Be clear in describing the uncertainty that exists: what is the possibility of this happening? (Giving this a rating helps prioritization.)
- ▶ Tailor the assessment to show the potential impact to the business. (Giving this a rating helps prioritization.)
- ▶ Base your assessment on the best information available at the time and record it (and update it regularly).
- ▶ Be systematic about how the risk is to be managed.

Take part in the discussion at www.cheeky-monkey.co/connect

Cheeky Monkey Wisdom

The management of risks is sometimes undervalued by project teams. It is your constant window on the outside world and should be a stark reminder that you aren't operating in isolation. Things change every day and if you don't keep tabs on that, you could be wasting precious time and energy on something that, at best, is no longer relevant or, at worst, means that you can no longer do what you had planned.

Step 38

Things that are stopping you

Things that are stopping you are issues and need resolution as quickly as possible. The process is the same as for risks, with the significant difference being that you need to act on and resolve them quickly. This time you know what has happened. Use the same structured collection process:

▶ Be specific, you know what is creating the issue.
▶ Tailor the plan to show the impact.
▶ Assign actions to an individual for resolution.
▶ Be systematic about how progress will be reported.

Take part in the discussion at www.cheeky-monkey.co/connect

Cheeky Monkey Wisdom

Project teams are usually comfortable collecting issues but the resolution of them can distract from actions that are on the project timeline. The project manager needs to work hard at keeping everyone working while issues are identified and resolved. This process might bring change; again, the project manager will weave that into the plan in a controlled way.

Step 39

Knowing when to say NO

Not everything will go the way that you want it to and, despite your best efforts, there may be things that affect your business transformation that are outside your control. You have to know at what point you are going to say 'no', and pull the plug on a project.

The longer projects go on, the more inconceivable it seems that you will stop; it's our natural tendency to plough on, make the best of it. Sometimes that is required but you need an objective mechanism to allow you to check your thinking and stop you from wasting resources. Changes that affect the scope of the project significantly also have to be questioned. It is better to close a project down and start a new one with a new scope than try and move the scope of a project already in play.

The objective measures will be in the project document as critical success factors (CSFs). These objective measures are things that must be delivered for the project to be successful. If changes (risks or issues) impact on the delivery of these CSFs, then the validity of the project must be challenged.

Take part in the discussion at www.cheeky-monkey.co/connect

Cheeky Monkey Wisdom

No one wants to be in a position where a project gets killed but it is better than limping along with a project that has been wounded. In my early days as a project manager, no one killed projects, the scope just changed and at some point the project no longer resembled what we had started out to do. Explaining the complicated project history to people that worked with us became more and more ridiculous and the project documentation became more complicated than it ever needed to be. Be brave: if it's not working, kill it. Learn the lesson and move on.

Step 40

Don't underestimate the people

As you progress through business transformation, the focus turns to the actions that result in the deliverables required to make the transformation come to life. There is a lot of focus on project management and the rational side of what needs to be achieved. We have touched on breaking habits and behavioural change and the dip that occurs when things get hard. People make business transformation successful: managing the people, and the emotions and politics that come with them, should not be underestimated.

If project management is about managing the rational, change management is about managing the emotions and politics.

The well-being and mental health of your employees is as important as the transformation deliverables. People are emotional and those emotions have a place at work; they can be harvested and used powerfully if they are understood and managed. Conversely, managed poorly they can be destructive.

Five things that you should always do:

- ▶ Be happy, energized, upbeat and smiley; it's contagious.
- ▶ Look for the good and use it to be positive about everything.
- ▶ Read the atmosphere. If it feels like something is wrong, it probably is. Don't ignore it: tease it out and manage it. Letting these things fester is bad.
- ▶ Meetings can be where explosions happen. Set the tone of meetings from the start; aim for calm, relaxed and consistent. You will be under time pressure but take time to find out how everyone is feeling and have a chat – you'll be amazed what you find out.
- ▶ Consciously manage the emotions of the team, otherwise they will take over.

Take part in the discussion at www.cheeky-monkey.co/connect

Cheeky Monkey Wisdom

People are primarily emotional, and passionate people are willing to show it. It is easier to manage passionate people than to tease out the emotions of people who believe you should not show your emotions in the workplace. You need to be self-aware to be able to manage emotions positively, which for some requires coaching. To be a great transformational leader, you need to be able to manage your own and others' emotions.

STORY 4: IT'S NOT ALWAYS A BED OF ROSES

Storyteller: Kevin Murphy, Managing and Creative Director, The Foundry Communications

The Foundry is one of the UK's top 30 design and top 25 pharmaceutical agencies.

Its growth is based on belief in strategic planning, creative problem-solving and strong client relationships. This is reflected in the agency's long-standing client base and new business acquisitions.

It creates internationally acclaimed work for clients including Molnlycke Health Care, Nike, Manchester United, Heineken, Matthew Clark, M & J Seafoods, Dechra Veterinary Products, Turkish Airlines, and Mamas and Papas.

The agency continues to successfully grow its offering across the board, none more so than in the digital area. The digital department is one of the company's fastest growing areas. It believes that websites and digital marketing are crucial to the success of clients' business objectives.

But above all, they are pragmatists and believe all clients have a requirement to 'sell today and build their brands for tomorrow'.

Me: People might read this book and think business transformation is something you can control but there is another side, one where things happen that are outside your control and transformation is forced on you. You my friend have been there and come out the other side and are willing to share that story with us.

Kevin: It will help for you to understand a bit of background. Educationally I was a late starter. I left school at 15 and went straight into work at a bakery; I became Mother's Pride youngest plant foreman. I thought that that was me for the rest of my life and not something that filled me delight.

Then a disaster happened in Florence; the Arno burst its banks and there was a cry for help as some of the world's greatest art works were in danger of being destroyed. It touched a nerve and I decided that I wanted to help, to be a painting restorer, naive I know, but my mind was set, I had a sense of purpose. It was the beginning of my personal transformation – I just didn't know it.

I rang the National Portrait Museum for some advice and spoke to a guy, he asked me to go down to London so he could advise me more. (It later turned out that 'the guy' was Sir Kenneth Clark which came as a bit of shock – what a great person to give me that time.) He explained the difficulties of being a painting restorer and how it was ten years of study and so on.

It didn't put me off, I took the plunge; I left a good job and went to university collecting some 'O' and 'A' Levels on the way! Manchester Art College would help tutor me in the first part of my new life in how to paint! However, it soon became apparent that is not what art college is all about. I started off wanting to paint but somehow slipped into design and advertising – a change of direction that affected the rest of my life.

My first job was with McCann-Erickson and my career grew very quickly as I moved around a couple of the large agencies and within three years I quadrupled my salary which was absolutely amazing; I couldn't believe it at the time.

I guess when you start to grow in yourself you see other people's frailties; eventually, I began to get frustrated. I started to think, 'You know what, I don't agree with what they are doing or saying and I'm certainly not signed into their vision – I need to do this my way'. So once again I took the plunge, I went part-time at McCann's. They gave me a three-day week which I had worked out was enough to cover my mortgage and three children. It meant I had seven nights and four days to start my own business – in a way I wanted it to be.

Again I was phenomenally lucky, I got to talk to the right people and work started flooding in, so much so that I realized I couldn't do it on my own. I met another like-minded freelance person and went into partnership with him. The company became amazingly successful and cash rich.

In 1992, it became clear that my partner and I had a different vision. He was a traditionalist, and I guess I wasn't. I was absolutely convinced that the Apple Mac would be the way forward and would change the way advertising was currently being produced in a dramatic way (apart from the creative process obviously). It had so much potential.

My partner didn't agree: he didn't want to invest in computers. I became frustrated very quickly and decided to close the business and follow my own vision.

On a working trip to New Zealand I can remember jotting down names of the most talented people I knew working in Manchester at the time and thought how brilliant would it be if I could pull them altogether, what an amazing offering, all these talented people with a new technology, a new way of doing things. Obviously finances would be the issue but once again I took the plunge.

Getting out of my partnership was a bit like a divorce, but not wanting to slow my vision I gave my partner more or less everything, and I was away.

At the same time I approached the ten names I had jotted down, people who I admired enormously in different areas of our business. Nine of them wanted to be part of my vision, I can't begin to tell you how incredibly flattering that is.

I had a bit of money and a bank overdraft of £100,000 so everything seemed rosy. We converted a cellar which was to be our office – from day one we looked and sounded something new. The energy and spirit in the company was phenomenal.

We had some start-up issues, the biggest one being a change of bank manager: within a month of start-up we had a new one and my bank overdraft went from £100,000 to nil overnight. We were really fortunate that two huge projects came along that kept the company going.

But the company went from strength to strength, voted Design Agency of the Year, Client Company of the Year, lots of awards and international recognition came in for the creative work and strategies we produced. I couldn't see where we could go wrong and my personal career graph continued to spiral upwards.

Our largest client at the time asked us to open an office in Scotland. Our existing contract was worth £2m, we were offered an extra £1.5m if we set up a local office in Edinburgh. I did a presentation and met their board (which was a bit daunting at the time). During the meeting it became apparent that if we didn't create a local office we would not get the additional budget and we would also lose the £2m we already had – it was a no-brainer of an offer, we all shook hands on the deal. I remember walking on air to the airport.

I could again only see the company going from strength to strength. By this time we employed 48 people and to support the office in Edinburgh we employed another 12 people. You can do the sums – that is a big overhead, a lot of birds in the nest that need feeding. And then disaster …

Within weeks of opening it became apparent that the promised extra spend was not forthcoming. Not only that, but our existing £2m contract was not coming through either.

I went in to see the then chairman (whom I later became very good friends with) who explained the situation his company was in: there was a massive slump in the economy and their marketplace; marketing budgets had been cut virtually overnight.

Obviously we had made a massive commitment to this company, but we stuck it out for a few months in the blind belief this was a temporary hiccup, otherwise I wouldn't have been called to that joyous meeting in the first place. But it wasn't.

My company went into liquidation. For the first time my career graph plummeted – from top to bottom. I was now a long way back in my dreams, further than when I was a baker. I was driving back from Scotland when the bank informed me they were pulling the plug there and then. I didn't even have money to put petrol in my car. My sister drove up with a couple of cans so I could get home.

This was the worst point of my whole life. I had never suffered this kind of loss; it affected me both personally and professionally. No bank, cheque book, no credit card and as it turned out no real friends. I learnt the stigma of losing a company especially such a successful one: as MD it was my fault, I never got anything written down, and a shake of the hands doesn't fix it in the corporate world.

You are dropped very quickly because you are deemed to be a loser, your friends turn out to be acquaintances, and you are on your own like never before.

Truthfully, I found myself walking down the back streets to get to Manchester just in case anyone bumped into me, I was that embarrassed. It is very difficult to explain that emotion. Yes, many of the large agencies offered me good roles within their companies, but I was torn.

And then, out of the blue I received a phone call from the chairman of the multinational. He explained how important our team was to his company and how sorry he was to learn of our demise. He said in order to keep a small part of our team together his company would lend me personally £50,000 to start again (paid back monthly). He felt an injustice had been done and he wanted to right it, but nonetheless, what an amazing gesture. I thought about his offer for a nano second and accepted it.

However, the emotional effects stayed with me, in fact secretly it still does. It was mainly because I had lost confidence in myself and felt I had let so many people down. However, despite that we opened an office above a tailor's shop, full of damp, paper coming off the walls, a smelly pink carpet, but at least it was somewhere to start again.

I chose to go into partnership with Ian who I worked with, even in this despair I could see (in media terms) another change coming, but I felt I couldn't do this on my own any more and Ian was/is a digital guru.

We had already designed a few websites and I could see that the industry was going to go through another revolution. We both had the same values and he was ready to have another shot at creating a difference.

The truth is, you can have a vision, but you need fantastic people around you. My philosophy has always been, try to employ people who are better than you or who have the potential to be. You can't go wrong if you find people like that.

Fortunately everything has gone really well since setting up with Ian and we've grown again. The company is again winning awards for its marketing strategies, its digital prowess, its creative excellence, its people and once again it is being recognized internationally for its overall capabilities.

I have to pinch myself sometimes and think how can it be that this little company, which now employs 28 people, works on a global scale with clients all over Europe, America? It's very flattering to be working alongside this team of people.

Me: So where do you go from here?

Kevin: I guess in my career I've hit all the pinnacles I wanted to achieve, voted Entrepreneur of the Year last year and so on and so forth. I'm 60 now and if I'm lucky I've got another 20 years, so I'm thinking about what next.

Me: In terms of transformation, if I take you back to when things were going well, did you business plan? Were you always searching forward in terms of transformation in the business as I assume it was always positive, always looking to improve, and always looking to take the next step?

Kevin: Yes, you can't stand still. My watershed was reading a book called *Differentiate or Die* [by Jack Trout]; the light turned on inside and I understood how everything I learnt over the years had a focus. It really pointed out and reaffirmed to me that all companies or brands should have a point of difference, that's why they grow and attract custom.

I knew that our business was no different, you have to have a long-term vision, yes it will change along the way, but at least you know a direction to follow.

And I recognize that in other client businesses, sometimes the successful ones (no matter how big) lose sight of what made them great. They lose sight of their point of difference. Successful start-ups normally have that difference but in truth many don't always see it in themselves, they are driven by the novelty of success and lose sight of their long-term direction. You can expand that to new product launches or older established brands. It's always comes back to the same basic principle – differentiation.

Our job is to go into companies and find it again or simply create it. Sometimes it's the people that are their point of difference, sometimes it's the product, sometimes you have to dig very deeply, but in my experience it's always there.

I also realized that in our own company we have to move with the times, for example, we were the first company in Manchester to go completely with Apple Macs in 1993. We were talked about; people said that we were breaking the rules; traditional thinkers who depended on us in an old-fashioned sense didn't like what we were doing, but I had to look to the future.

The reason for employing people the way we did and do is because they all brought or bring a point of difference with them, you have to be amorphous. You have to continually change and challenge yourself to grow.

The Foundry continues to thrive, but we are now going through another series of changes (transformation). They are planned, they are not happening by accident. Sometimes you've just got to have the vision and look a bit further than next week or next year.

It's absolutely obvious that traditional media is changing and has been for a couple of years. We've been fortunate to be in a place to keep abreast and even lead in some of these digital developments. Once again there is a revolution in digital communications and it will never stand still. The impact social media has had in a global sense is truly breathtaking; ignore it at your peril.

We're helping clients (holding hands in some cases), developing communications in an inventive way, guiding them through pitfalls, but breaking new ground together. Now more than ever we are sharing in each other's vision.

Planning for change is a constant; it can happen in small increments or wholesale changes but it has to happen – if it doesn't you're dead in the water.

Me: When you went bust, what was it that you held onto to say 'Okay, yeah, well this has happened but I can now reinvent myself again and come out the other side'? What was the thing that made that possible?

Kevin: It wasn't really like that. I got offered a lot of opportunities and I did go to talk to people about some high-profile positions. The only reason that I wanted to set up again was that despite how desperate I felt personally, I just couldn't see myself working for anybody else. It wasn't pre-ordained; I didn't have the self-belief that I could just start where I left off.

I also realized I wasn't a bad person and again in hindsight I have learned enormously from that experience. Nothing is wasted in life if you learn from it.

Me: There must have been something in your toolkit, where you could dig deep and think right, despite all of the emotion and despite the lack of confidence you knew you could start again?

Kevin: If you run your own business, you realize that what makes it happen is your determination and hopefully others around you pick up on that. Once I got over the emotional aspect of what happened, determination was the driver.

I took all my children out one evening and apologized to them for not being around enough whilst they were growing up. I declared to them that I used to say, 'I'm doing all this for you, so you can have a better start to life than me. I'm going to make sure you get to university, blah, blah, blah' That night I owned up to the fact that it was always about my own personal need to achieve. Their response was so unexpected, 'Dad you are you, that's why we love you, as far as we are aware we have not missed out on anything, you've been there when we needed you.' So I had a cry and thanked God for having three wonderful children.

The important thing that I realized after the company went bust, despite how I was feeling about myself, was that I had to do it again for me. I've been very fortunate it worked out.

Me: How would you define transformation? What does it mean to you?

Kevin: Transformation is a continual process. Transformation isn't a single thing that happens. You don't go from A to B; you have a road of transformation, it's not always the straight line you expect.

There's a little wine bar across from us and it changes hands every year. It's very successful, then the customer base falls off a little at a time and then it closes and changes hands to another start-up with a point of difference. It shouldn't be like that.

As I say transformation is a continual process. What the bar had to recognize was why it was being successful and for what reason. And alongside that it had to look forward, keep reinventing itself because there will always be competitors with new more exciting offerings (easy for me to say observing across the square).

All of us are customers, we like to try new; when it's a good experience we return, but reinvention is the key to a continual relationship with a company or a brand. You don't have to do it in a big way, you can do it in small ways or increments. Decor, people, brand extensions, there are so many ways to do this, but one thing is for sure, change has to take place and companies have to find their own way of being remarkable in some way big or small. To labour the point – they have to acknowledge the need for transformation.

Section 5
Looking, Learning and Moving On

FEEDBACK

Step 41

Don't get lost

By now you should have got at least two messages:

- ▶ Transformation is a journey.
- ▶ A programme or projects deliver change.

When it's all going on and things are changing and the business is reacting, you need to make sure there are points when you come back, establish true north and make sure you are still heading where you want to go. It is very easy to get lost.

The business plan is true north. It sets out financially what you need to do and what you think you will get in return. We need to make sure we are mapping our achievements back to that at regular points. You need to make sure that you know how the highs and lows are affecting your cash position.

If you have a complex business you will have lots of accounting lines to establish, but for the purposes of focused thinking it's simple: you have things you have to pay for to deliver the product and service you offer; in return, people pay you money for that. There is, of course, a gap between the two transactions.

When you go through transformation different things happen that can affect your cash position and you need to keep track of those. It sounds obvious, common sense and generally people do write this down. What is common is the lack of understanding about timing and when everyone is busy and it feels like you are making great progress, you can trip up because your timing is out. To make sure you are still heading in the right direction and in terms of timing you are OK, you need to be conscious of the following:

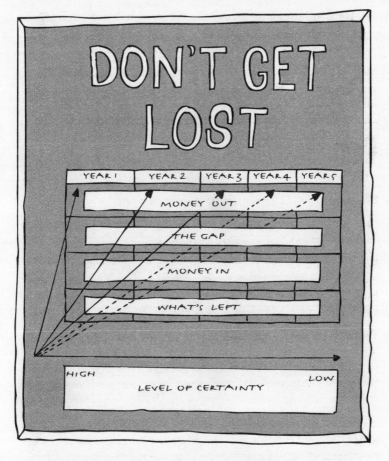

- ▶ You are investing in change – that costs money even if you are using your own people to do everything. You must keep track of investment costs.
- ▶ If you are using your own people there might be some business disruption during the change. It's hard to do everything you did before plus the change – something will give.
- ▶ Was your plan to keep all your customers happy? Are you putting some at risk to venture into a new market? There can be a lag in you finding out what they think, so you need to set alarms that give you an indication of how that's going.
- ▶ Have things changed that you have no control over? What difference is that making?

▶ If you are in it for the long game (3–5 years), will your funds get you there? Do you need to think about short-term goals to ensure that you will be around to see the long-term ones to fruition?

You need to do this with the people responsible for the money coming into the business (sales), the money going out of the business (every other function) and your finance person. Don't be tempted to do this with your finance person alone. They can only tell you that $10 - 15 = -5$. They can't tell you how to make it $+5$.

Take part in the discussion at www.cheeky-monkey.co/connect

Cheeky Monkey Wisdom

Focusing on the numbers provides the cold shower that you need at key points in the process. It's not just about making sure you have enough money in the bank either. Some of the worst decisions are made by businesses that don't need to worry about money. Having a financial buffer gives a level of comfort that makes people wasteful.

Step 42

Keep looking, listening and learning

It's never really over; it's just another phase in the journey. The world will not stop while you are going through transformation – though it would be so nice if it would and it would make the process far simpler. Keeping the mindset that it's about continual improvement should help you keep the picture of product and service lifecycles in your mind, while your projects are delivering discrete components of change.

Take part in the discussion at www.cheeky-monkey.co/connect

Cheeky Monkey Wisdom

When we train people on delivering new product introductions, we get the team to hold a bag of money. They have to split the investment the business is making across the key stages of the product development and implementation process. We then ask the team to tell us whether it's easy for the executive team to say 'stop' or 'no' at each decision point. At the start of the process, the decision to stop is easy (little money has been spent). As we move through the phases and the money bag gets emptier, the ability to say 'no' gets harder. Each time we get to pre-launch (the stuff is in the warehouse and it's ready to be shipped out), everyone says 'you never say no at this point, all the money has been spent, you might as well just send it'. They stop thinking about the outside world and are completely focused on their project. The damage that can be done to a brand because you stopped looking, listening and learning about what is happening outside can outstrip all of your projects costs. Remember New Coke?

Step 43

....

Projects have to end

If you have followed our process then each of your projects will have clear deliverables and an end date. Regular updates and change control will make it easy to see if they are on track and when they will finish. Under pressure to finish there are two things that frequently get squeezed at the end, a completely false economy:

▶ testing
▶ training.

Although projects should never go past their sell-by date, neither should you trip just before the finish line in order to finish. Testing and training are all about sustainability: get these wrong and your project will be amazing, but its ability to transition to business as usual will be hampered.

It doesn't really matter what project you are delivering, these two components are valid:

▶ product: concept testing, technical testing, consumer acceptance, market testing, communication testing, sales training, consumer training, etc.
▶ process: testing to see if it works, training to make sure people can use it
▶ system: testing to see if it works, training to make sure people can use it
▶ structure: testing to see if it works, training to make sure people can work within it.

Validating the deliverables will help you assess if they are sustainable. There may be a gap between you finishing the project and knowing if the change has been successful – that is a risk that should be managed post-project so that action can be taken if it looks like assumptions made are not going to be realized. Don't take your eye off the ball too soon.

Take part in the discussion at www.cheeky-monkey.co/connect

Cheeky Monkey Wisdom

We managed a project for a company that was willing to invest significant sums of money to deliver a new range of products to the market but not to test the concepts thoroughly or prove the route to market. It was a significant concern of the project team as the project was nearing completion but they were under pressure to complete. The project was hailed a success because all the deliverables had been achieved on time and in budget and projected sales numbers built into the business plan. The route to market failed. The impact was not felt for another 12 months. It took another 12 months for the business to review what had gone wrong, by which time the shelf life of the product had expired.

Step 44

End-of-project review

A project's end should signal a business's new beginning. The end-of-project review should be a place where we review what has actually happened versus what we planned. We should also be handing the baton on to those who have daily responsibility for making sure this change is now part of the everyday world.

This is the start of the continuous learning cycle and you need quality information to be circulated widely so that the culture starts to transform. This needs to be dealt with sensitively but honestly because the best learning comes from the things that didn't go well and on-one really wants to be associated with those. It can also be a bit of a downer to focus on the things that didn't go so well, especially when people are tired, have normally gone above and beyond to deliver the project, and would like to relish the moment of completion. Think the format through ahead of time and be the facilitator for the end of project story.

Take part in the discussion at www.cheeky-monkey.co/connect

Cheeky Monkey Wisdom

Projects are an opportunity to work outside the constraints of the day-to-day business structure to deliver change effectively and efficiently. They are normally intense and people tend to give you over and above what is expected. How you end a project will affect how they feel about tackling the next one and doing it all over again. Each component of the end-of-project review needs attention and planning: Where you are going to do it? How long will it take (including some relaxing team time)? How will you elicit the learning in the most positive way? How will you make people feel looked after and cared for? The review should cement a positive experience for the people involved and leave them wanting more.

Step 45

....

Next chapter in the story

As projects finish delivering their tangibles and lessons learnt, all the information needs to be pegged back to the transformation story so people can see progress and understand the chapters in the journey. When you tell your first story, there is a need for a certain amount of blind faith from the audience because you will be saying 'we don't know what we don't know, but this is the plan'. Each project completing adds some facts, 'this is what we do know and this is how it affects our journey'.

This is also the opportunity to give some of the heroes their five minutes in the sunshine. Getting the people who have been part of the projects talking to the business is always motivational for everyone, especially when they share the highs and lows. There isn't any better confirmation of an empowered workforce than everyone seeing and hearing from them.

The big fish of the business has to be there, supporting and adoring what they have done, and making the final link to the next chapter.

Take part in the discussion at www.cheeky-monkey.co/connect

This is when transformation starts to take hold. Making sessions like this part of the normal business structure shows everyone that when the business says it's going to do something it means it. So often in businesses if you are not part of a project team you don't get to hear anything past the inaugural story, and the rumour mill takes the place of anything official. There are always projects to be delivered and you want your workforce to see that if you put yourself out there and get involved, there are rewards in terms of recognition and relationships with different people in the business, generally more sought after than money.

Step 46

Coming home

Projects need to transition into business as usual for them to deliver sustainable change. This can be hard on the project team who naturally are protective over their work at this stage. The transition is not only about the work; the people who have been working in the project team need to transition back to the business.

The project manager and programme manager (if you have one) should be talking to the business about this as you enter the final quarter of the plan so that you can talk to the project team members as their minds start to drift back to what they were doing before.

Many people change when they have worked on a transformation project – hopefully they have grown in themselves, learnt new skills and ways of working, and generally yearn for more than they had before. Sometimes it's possible to make that happen within your business and sometimes the timing is not right. Whatever the situation, you need to recognize it is not just about what you want, it's also about what they want and having an adult conversation about it is a good start.

Take part in the discussion at www.cheeky-monkey.co/connect

Cheeky Monkey Wisdom

If you have dedicated project team members to long-term projects, then this discussion and transition is crucial because they may have lost touch with their 'old' job and the chances are things will have changed. People do not want to see that working on projects is a shortcut to the door with exit above it.

Step 47

Celebrate success

People are still generally modest and will shy away from the moment where they are being praised and told that they have done well. They may be standing in front of you physically when you are telling them but internally most people will be dismissing what is being said – it's just human nature. When you put people who have worked together in a situation where, as a team, they are taking credit, something amazing happens. It seems easier for people to enjoy that moment of self-promotion in a crowd and they enjoy flaunting their bad ass self!

For me, celebrations should be individual and significant to the people in the team. The care taken to think about that and demonstrating to the people in the team that you know them adds a personal dimension that is worth the effort.

Basics:

▶ It should include an indulgent gesture (leaving work an hour early, taxi fare paid for, staying a night in a luxury hotel); it can work within the constraints of your budget; it is more the act of doing something that doesn't normally happen.
▶ It should include something that builds self-respect, and encourages people to think well of themselves.
▶ It magnifies the positive things that have happened.

Take part in the discussion at www.cheeky-monkey.co/connect

Cheeky Monkey Wisdom

Getting people to celebrate success at work is not always as easy as you would think. We seem to have got out of the habit and the frenetic lives people have outside of work seem to make some people groan at the thought of a night out, never mind a night away. Making it personal and significant helps to ebb that reaction away, and shows people that effort warrants returned effort. Just going to the pub and standing round the bar chatting might not deliver the basics, and small budgets require more creativity. Invest in it because they are worth it.

STORY 5: DUMPING THE TRADITIONAL FOR THE SOCIAL

Storyteller: Marc Lind, Senior VP Global Marketing, ARAS Corporation

ARAS is a global provider of enterprise software for what is referred to as Product Lifecycle Management (PLM) solutions. These help companies manage their product development, quality compliance, manufacturing, outsourcing and supply chain on a worldwide scale.

Me: You don't deliver PLM software the same way as the rest of the market, do you?

Marc: We are unique because we are the first provider of this type of software in an open source format which gives companies control over their own destiny in terms of the ability to manage the software, configure it for their specific operations and it transforms the business relationship between us the provider and the client company. We eliminate the licence cost and give them a predictable fixed cost structure. This is very different from the conventional manner of selling this type of enterprise software.

We really have unique innovation around the technology which allows us to compete against much larger companies. We have put together a special sauce so to speak, and it really gives us and our clients a benefit.

Me: You did start out like everyone else though?

Marc: Ten years ago we decided to go to market the same way everybody else had which was selling the software, having a large sales force and trying to convince people that they should use our system as opposed to say a system from one of the alternative providers out there.

We found that the world was changing and that companies really wanted to engage with a provider of these types of solutions in a different manner. That was something that took us some time to figure out because we were selling it in a traditional manner. We have since gone through a transformation process where we have done away with the sales teams and the high-cost salesmen and really moved to social media – a social marketing type of platform and engagement model for our customers and our company which is quite different and I can explain that as we go.

Me: You said that you saw that the world was changing and that your customers wanted something different, did you use any tools for that? How did you decide and then make the connection back to your own company?

Marc: We took a look at the overall software market in about 2005, 2006 timeframe and we had good growth. It certainly was not as if we were going to take over the industry and gain significant market share, we were growing incrementally. Our Board of Directors put it to the executive team what is the fastest path to profitable growth and a much higher growth rate.

As a management team we set out to study what was going on, particularly with the consumer and internet and look at how those changes in behaviour, changes in activity were trending towards the business market. That process actually took a couple of years and is still ongoing. We now consider ourselves a learning organization where we are constantly running tests and trying to identify what works and what doesn't, do more of what works and stop doing what isn't working.

Me: It must have been quite a moment when you were reviewing what was happening and looking for that path to growth and profitability when someone said 'We can do this better if we get rid of the sales force'?

Marc: Certainly, in fact there were a number of moments I would say. It was a process not an event.

Me: That I think would be quite interesting for people to understand that the route to more profitable growth was to get rid of the sales channel.

Marc: Yes. We were drawing conclusions as we were reviewing different segments of the market and mapping how those related to our market category. I can't say that we had an 'Aha' moment which was 'Get rid of the sales force', it was more like we began to think about the way our pricing and packaging was structured and then think about how that differentiated us and created value for our clients and prospective clients. Then what the implications were of going to market with this new structure and that really unfolded over the course of about 12 to 18 months.

It was quite interesting I would say there was never a unanimous 'This is the right answer.' We had a strong CEO who really had a tight grasp on the vision and would put stakes in the ground: 'We cannot forfeit this type of mission.' In doing so at various points in time along this year, year and a half, two year process, everyone in the organization at some point or another said 'No, this isn't going to work and we need to not do this', including the CEO himself, so it really was a process where there was strong leadership and then reinforcement across the team in times of uncertainty.

Me: I suppose there was a double whammy there because it wasn't only getting rid of the traditional sales channel but it was offering the product as open source, quite ballsy moves when it comes to financial planning?

Marc: Certainly, this also was not a decision that was just a moment in time. There are a lot of moving parts when you have an ongoing global business operation and with an investment community and shareholders with existing customers with a lot of structure in place. Our transformation meant that we needed to figure out a wide variety of things from the licensing and legal structures to the financial models and revenue models and business model, the fundamental 'How are you going to make money?' through to the operational and product aspects, and into the marketing sales and how we go to market.

All of these were moving parts over the course of this transformation, some of the things when we did throw the switch to move to this open source format we got right, some we obviously got wrong but we quickly adjusted. Other parts needed to be tweaked and refined and optimized. But overall we feel as if we have successfully transformed the business and just last year had over 100% growth in our subscription business, which is the core of our business model.

Me: It wasn't one eureka moment, this has been a progressive journey that you have taken. Did you forecast how long it would take for you to start seeing the benefits of these changes?

Marc: Absolutely. We had five-year financial models which were essential to our business planning. We had quite extensive economic analysis and financial modelling and sensitivity analysis on those models that we had done for different scenarios. We were overly optimistic in some areas while underestimating other areas. So on balance we were pretty close to our planning process especially, this might seem surprising, especially given the amount of change which has gone on because nobody including us saw the financial crisis and the ensuing global recession occurring in the 2008 timeframe.

Me: Absolutely. Despite that, when those things happened which actually no one forecast, did you find yourselves having to re-plan or did you just hold steady and watch how things played out?

Marc: Well we certainly took contingency measures and as a management team our executives each came up with plans related to their geographies and organizations that would be necessary for different scenarios depending on the length and the depth but we, I will say, we leaned into the punch. We saw the financial, not the financial crisis so much, that was the initial inception but the global recession we saw as an opportunity. We saw it as an opportunity to accelerate our growth. So we adjusted our plan to put in place a whole series of measures that would capitalize on these events as opposed to putting our heads in the sand.

Me: In terms of your use of social media, when did that start? In the UK it has been a very slow burn from a business perspective. We have gone through the last couple of years with people saying 'It will never catch on', to people realizing it is actually here to stay. Adoption of it has yet to peak really and tip over into a mass-used tool. What's your view on the uptake in the business community?

Marc: Well, as we went through the transformation process and were looking at the implications of our change in a business model, social media was beginning to catch on in the United States. It had already taken off in the consumer-oriented aspects where you had of course e-commerce and people were blogging. Facebook had started and was beginning to grow and YouTube was just taking off. We saw that this was moving at growth rates that were undeniable. You are talking about orders of magnitude in terms of adoption.

Now remember this is also primarily consumers and individuals as opposed to businesses. However, our planning assumptions were that the internet is not a fad, it is real and it is here to stay. As the global population of people and businesses continues to get connected that collaborative development, that social interaction and social media, that social networking was here to stay and is only going to continue to grow.

So really the only question is at what point in time will critical mass be achieved in any given industry? So from a business standpoint we saw early adopters in the software world, in the electronics world. Whereas if you look at vertical industries, industries like defence, like industrial equipment, they were much slower to adopt and I think are really just coming online and becoming more savvy and engaged today.

Me: Very similar to what is happening here. In fact I think fear is the thing that grips most of the business world even now and it is of course the dichotomy that social media is meant to be social and I think businesses still struggle to be social in an unforced way.

Marc: I definitely agree with that. I think that what is happening and there are a lot of people out there saying this, but I am seeing it first hand is that people in their private lives, business leaders and managers and individual contributors are going home and their kids, their family members are all interacting and they are using the internet. They are buying books on amazon.com, they are going out and they are shopping and having items sent to relatives for the holidays. So they are using the tools in their personal lives, they are just not quite certain how to apply them in the business world. You see it beginning to come to fruition that incrementally you can see 'oh I could apply a discussion thread here', 'we could take advantage of a blog to get our position on an issue or issues and to promote our product' and that type of thing.

Those are exactly the types of steps that we took here. It wasn't as if at ARAS we just said 'oh it's going to be all social'. What we did was really look at which tool applied and supported what scenario, particularly with respect to marketing and sales. This is something that I take very seriously and have driven throughout our organization.

Social media, social marketing, social networking, this is not something that you assign to someone, say a marketing person who is a low-level individual. Social is really about communicating or interacting or as I put it communicating with competence and when you are doing that and engaging with clients and prospective clients you are really talking about issues. I think this connects directly back to the direct sales force.

Not to put it in too unkind a way but for the kind of software that we are dealing with, very complex, large scale, organizationally and collaboration oriented within a global company, I have yet to meet a company or customer or an executive who is dying to talk to their software sales representative.

That person is typically the gatekeeper and is typically the person that has the least trust with the client and customer. What the company and the customer, what they really want is to talk to the experts. Those are the engineers, those are the application specialists, those are the executives. So by removing the sales person from the equation you actually achieve a much healthier relationship with your customers and you are able to have a higher level of trust and engagement with them. You move from the customer keeping the information away from you to a kind of 'Well, here is what we are really trying to do and we are trying to figure out whether your software and your organization can support us in achieving these goals.'

I believe that this is the model of engagement in the 21st century here and that companies who use social media and understand that it is not someone else's job, that it really is part of all the experts' jobs across the organization and that it is a conversational format, are going to excel and achieve otherwise disproportionate growth.

Me: Do you think though it is going to take the next generation of managers to actually achieve that?

Marc: This has been a point that is brought up quite frequently; I see it online a lot. Personally I don't believe that will be the case.

I believe that because people, even people who are resistant to the online experience are using the tools at home because of the convenience factor, because of the ability to do things that they otherwise wouldn't be able to accomplish, like shopping, like reading reviews on products.

These days I don't buy a product unless I can go and research it and find out what other users are saying online, people who are actually using the product whether we are talking about a camera or TV, whether we are talking about tyres for my car or a new car itself. In my personal life I am very tuned in to wanting actual information from people who already have experience with the product that I am looking at.

So that is just an example of the types of things and experiences I believe that even established and one might say older personnel in the business environment, they are doing that today. I believe it just takes a little more time for them to figure out where these types of tools are applicable in their organization than say someone who is the younger generation maybe just coming out of college.

It is coming too quickly for people to resist, they are participating whether they acknowledge it or not and so the real question is 'What do we use to support our different processes and what are we trying to achieve?' So it is really goal and results oriented. You just have to think about 'what am I trying to do?' 'what are we trying to achieve as an organization'? and 'what can I use to support these goals?'

Me: ARAS has been heavily involved in pushing the business forward in a very progressive way, in a way that is in advance of general business thinking at the moment. You are already way ahead of the curve and

have been for some time. Do you constantly plan for transformation even though you know that you have probably not hit tipping point with what you have already got out in the market?

Marc: Well, certainly we are pretty pragmatic here, we are practical. What we are doing is constantly looking forward in our business and setting goals. We have some pretty aggressive growth goals and we are thinking about this in terms of network effect.

The next phase for us is to expand this from what we have been doing out in our customer and our broader community base, the corporate community. As well as that, through the partner network we deal with a whole ecosystem of companies that are value-added integrators, who help with deployment, who create add-on solutions to our system and our platform. We believe that for us as we scale to really help these organizations to get it and be progressive in their own right with respect to engaging with clients using social techniques, social networking, this is going to be beneficial.

So in other words take the load off of our shoulders and distribute it out across the global network that we are dealing with on a daily basis.

Me: It is clear that the customer, your customer is at the core of all of your transformation, but you are not trying to meet an existing need. It seems like you are trying to give your customer an alternative, something that they haven't actually thought about but that takes away the frustration and the pain associated with dealing with the traditional software community. So instead of just trying to meet a need which your product does, you are trying to make it a more positive overall experience. Is that right?

Marc: I guess in part. We are certainly laser-focused on customer needs, customer problems, solving challenges that global companies have in trying to deal with new product development and business processes across their product life cycle. In the greater say world view, we are looking at the manner in which these types of solutions have been provided to companies in the past and I will just say it has been quite mono-dimensional and convincing.

It is like people think they are selling the silver bullet or they are buying the silver bullet where the salesman goes in and says there is a sales presentation, there is some dog and pony and tap dancing and fancy slides and lots of brochures and then magic will happen if you spend a few million dollars and buy this thing that I am selling for software. We believe that that is not a sustainable, not a growth model moving forward.

What companies want is actually to have a partner, a corporate partner that they can work with through thick and thin and that there is a level of transparency.

A sales representative's job is to keep information away and to only provide the information that they want the customer to hear. Whereas in a social network, social media way, particularly with open source and the type of software we are dealing with, the marketplace, companies can find out about what problems and challenges the software can solve for them, they can engage either online or in person and it is a balanced relationship where the risk is shared. So you are moving forward to accomplish goals together and this means that you have a much healthier relationship and you are actually teaming whereas before it is kind of vendor–customer type of adversarial relationship.

So we think that social media is one tool, one platform, one combination of tools I should say that supports this overall change in the way companies are engaging and partnering here into the future.

Me: So if you had to define transformation for the people that will be reading this book, what would be a definition you would give?

Marc: Well that is an interesting question. I think that like many definitions they are situation dependent. From a transformation, a business transformation standpoint, the way that I think about it personally is that we are talking about continuously improving, adjusting, optimizing, adapting your business and your structures, your pricing, how you go to market, your revenue structures, your goals even to capitalize on opportunities in the marketplace.

I think it was Charles Darwin who said that it is not survival of the strongest, it is survival of the fittest and the fittest are those who are most capable of adapting. I think that that is going to be a watch word and transformation is going to be the mantra of the 21st century. It is really continuous transformation.

Me: Is there is anything else you want to say?

Marc: I encourage anybody who is reading this: the thing that will stop you from transforming your business is fear. It also can be a motivator for you to transform your business.

Sometimes when you see change coming you have to run at fear and that I believe is going to be an important thing to consciously understand here in the 21st century as we see more and more volatility in the markets and more and more opportunity emerging faster and faster. So that is just my own perspective and my two cents, take it for what it's worth but go forth and be successful.

Section 6
Science

Step 48

....

Brain training

Ever had those days when you wish you could split yourself into two? Well, you can, or your mind anyway. Nobel Prize winner Roger Sperry conducted something called the Split Brain Experiment where he proved that each side of our brain works independently joined by a cable that allows us to move from one side to the other quickly. Most of us are lazy when it comes to what our own personal computer can do for us, diminished further by our reliance on machines that can do the thinking for us.

Nintendo obviously found a brilliant way of combining the two, sales rocketed and your mum and dad can be found on the sofa with a DS (I never thought I would see the day). Japanese scientist Dr Ryuta Kawashima, creator of the Brain Training games, didn't take any of the profit he was entitled to for designing the games, claiming work was his hobby. Put your money away, follow in the doctor's footsteps, you can get all the brain training you need from work – and it can be just as fun!

There is a bit of science involved to make us conscious of our brain, so here goes:

▶ The potential of the human brain is infinite.
▶ We have an unlimited capacity to learn (just think of all the really intelligent people in the world – their brains are not full and they can still learn more).
▶ There are two sides to our brain: left and right. In today's world it is thought that left dominates and you don't have to be a genius to see why: left = safe, right = risk-taking.

▶ Our conscious mind can only focus on data from one side at a time but can switch from side to side very quickly. In business transformation you use that switching, that mental agility, all the time.

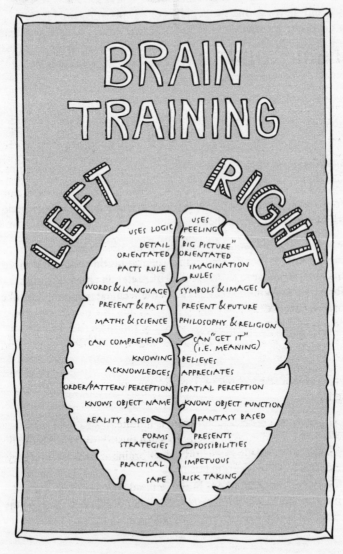

Source: Roger Sperry 1973

It is a constant workout for your brain and in my experience it is something that some people are better at than others, which doesn't mean that everyone can't do it, just that some people need to use things to help train their brain how to work at its full potential.

Which side of your brain dominates you? Think about the way you work and they way that the people around you work and identify the decisions you make and actions you take with the corresponding sides of your brain. Do you let one side of your brain dominate? How often do you make a decision or take action that involved thinking from the other side of your brain?

There is no right or wrong here – the exercise is to make you conscious. Business transformation requires equal parts of left and right brain and the ability to consciously travel between the two. If you find it hard to do it all in your head, write things down, mind-map things, and make the connections on paper as an aid to getting your mind to be conscious about what is going on.

Why is this important? Objectivity. Independent of mind, unbiased, free of emotion and prejudice – how can you be objective if you are not conscious of why you are thinking what you think?

Bringing objectivity into your transformation is the glue that keeps it all hanging together in the right way. It creates an environment that everyone sees is fair and that has a phenomenal effect on the way people behave.

Take part in the discussion at www.cheeky-monkey.co/connect

Cheeky Monkey Wisdom

Good news for those worried about Alzheimer's: delivering business transformation is better than any brain training game on the market. Put down that Nintendo and pick up a business to transform!

Step 49

Behaviour

Behaviour is a combination of science and magic. There are many things written by brilliant people in this area and they can boost your knowledge. However, to progress and really understand the behaviour of someone, you have to get to know them and that's more about magic.

Now I am going to go through the complex subject of behaviour and what you are looking to change. We will end up agreeing that you have to get to know the people you work with, but there are so many layers to this debate and we have to go through them to understand what you are trying to achieve.

We are all individuals who have the same components inside but not wired up the same way. As we evolve we are subjected to so many things that have an effect on how we see the world and how we choose to behave in it. It is always changing. Behavioural change isn't hard; it happens every day. Changing someone's behaviour to the way you want them to behave, now that is hard because you have to convince them that it's better for them to make the change – not just you.

Is it your behaviour that needs to change? Will that change have a domino effect on the whole team?

You need to challenge whether you want to change the way someone behaves or what they do. Is it the way they do something that needs to change or what they are doing that needs to change?

And then of course there is personality. If change is required at an individual level, is it really about the way that person is behaving or does their personality clash with those around them?

Is this about an individual's behaviour you are trying to change or the behaviour of a collective group that have to work together? Understanding and changing behaviour in global teams is the best brain training you can get.

What we already know:

▶ At an individual level, our behaviour is judged by social norms and people describe it as common, usual, acceptable or unacceptable against that social framework (government policy, rules, etiquette) and we try and regulate behaviour by using controls (fines, jail, being told off).

▶ That follows through into the workplace where what is acceptable and unacceptable is controlled by the management hierarchy.

▶ It's common for people to behave differently in a group situation than they do individually because personality types come into the mix.

▶ The way we control the individuals that come and work for us has a direct impact on their behaviour at an individual level and perhaps more importantly at a group level. Personality heightens or dampens that effect.

▶ It is impossible to know how people are going to react in different situations and to different things. There are so many variables, but we can generalize: e.g. be dismissive of an idea shared publicly and the chances are that person will think twice about shouting out again. It's not rocket science.

Behaviour in the workplace is characterized in the main by two things:

▶ **The leaders.** They set the rules and create the environment that everyone else is going to work in. Things like dress code, working flexibility (hours, workplace, etc.), openness of communication, reward systems (and the fairness of), trust, status-orientated perks (car parking, class of travel, hotels, etc.) all create the environment that people's behaviour is influenced by.

▶ **The culture of the people that work in it** (not to be confused with the culture of the organization). In our increasingly global workplace, this has an increasing influence.

How you act as leaders re-enforces a perception one way or the other. If you say one thing and do another, it changes people's perception and as a result their behaviour, regardless of the environment, rules and culture.

If you are reading this and thinking 'see there is nothing I can do, I am not one of the leaders and they will never change', you are wrong: that is not where I am going with this.

Every one of us has the ability to influence behavioural change by being the change we want to see (Gandhi, of course). All the greats have done it. Did Nelson Mandela leave Robben Island affected by how people had behaved with him, changed by his environment? No, he took office knowing that he had to be the change he wanted to see first (for inspiration watch *Invictus*). If you really believe there is a need for behaviour to change to deliver your transformation, then it starts with you.

If you become the change you want to see and nothing changes, then this may not be the right environment for you.

We are all different: take some time to get to know the people around you, figure out what makes them who they are and why they behave in the way that they do. Embrace the differences and create teams that will benefit from the diversity – that's why you employed them in the first place.

Take part in the discussion at www.cheeky-monkey.co/connect

Cheeky Monkey Wisdom

During a global PLM implementation covering ten countries, we knew that behaviour needed to change for the solution to work. It wasn't about the individuals. The point of failure was the behaviour between the teams delivering the work and the management teams. Without changing the behaviour that existed in that relationship, the new process and technology would never return on its substantial investment.

Step 50

Culture

'We need to include cultural change' is part of every discussion we have with our clients and my heart sinks at the point that it is mentioned. This is a very complex area, getting more complicated by the increasingly global nature of our work. At its most basic level culture is shared values and practices, so in the workplace that should be easy to change, right?

At a superficial level, yes. Go through a mission, vision, values exercise and agree what you share and how you are going to practise that.

The problem is that your organization today is full of people conforming to the current culture and it's not static. Every time a new person joins they bring a piece of their own culture to the mix. The environment brings changes that affect our culture.

Understanding the culture you have is of course the starting point. How do people act? What do they do? What is the common behaviour? You need to listen to people inside and outside the business and get their honest view about what it is like to interact with the company. Look at what is written about you.

Once you have an understanding of what the culture is today, then ask yourself what is it you want to change and why.

Take part in the discussion at www.cheeky-monkey.co/connect

Cheeky Monkey Wisdom

There can be a mismatch between what you say your organizational culture is and what it actually is. Actions speak louder than words when it comes to culture.

Step 51

Step 51

Mission and vision

Mission = why do you exist today?

Vision = where are you going?

Mission

The mission should be short, memorable and inspiring. It's all about being market-focused and what you want to be remembered for.

See if you can name the company from these mission statements (you can find the answers at the end of this step):

1 To organize the world's information and make it universally accessible and useful.
2 Make food good.
3 Be the world's best quick service restaurant experience. Being best means providing outstanding quality, service, cleanliness and value so that we make every customer in every restaurant smile.
4 To be the earth's most customer centric company; to build a place where people can come to find and discover anything they might want to buy online.
5 To refresh the world. To inspire moments of optimism and happiness. To create value and make a difference.

These statements communicate the culture of the business internally and externally so it is important not to rush them; get people involved and get them right.

There is no better way than to brainstorm and use sticky notes so you can move things around and play different scenarios before choosing the one most suited to you.

Things to think about:

▶ behaviour in the business and how that translates
▶ inspirational reasons your employees and customers deal with you
▶ things that people in the business and customers are proud of
▶ culture: there needs to be a match.

Vision

The vision is where you are going so it needs to be:

▶ all about the future
▶ clear and visible
▶ audacious
▶ descriptive
▶ 5+ years in horizon.

Coca-Cola

Our vision serves as the framework for our Roadmap and guides every aspect of our business by describing what we need to accomplish in order to continue achieving sustainable, quality growth.

▶ People: Be a great place to work where people are inspired to be the best they can be.
▶ Portfolio: Bring to the world a portfolio of quality beverage brands that anticipate and satisfy people's desires and needs.
▶ Partners: Nurture a winning network of customers and suppliers, together we create mutual, enduring value.
▶ Planet: Be a responsible citizen that makes a difference by helping build and support sustainable communities.
▶ Profit: Maximize long-term return to shareowners while being mindful of our overall responsibilities.
▶ Productivity: Be a highly effective, lean and fast-moving organization.

Google

1 Focus on the user and all else will follow.
2 It's better to do one thing really well.
3 Fast is better than slow.
4 Democracy on the web works.
5 You don't need to be at your desk to need an answer.
6 You can make money without doing evil.
7 There's always more information out there.
8 The need for information crosses all borders.
9 You can be serious without a suit.
10 Great just isn't good enough.

THINGS TO THINK ABOUT:

▶ You are looking to energize people with the vision.
▶ It should contain the things that matter to the business, its employees and customers.
▶ It should provide direction and purpose.
▶ It must be clear and easy to understand.
▶ Make it ambitious, because it's bridging the gap between today and the future.

These statements are only worth something if they are alive. The reason for choosing the examples I have is that the companies are recognizable through those words. It is more than a set of carefully chosen words, it's what the company believes in and what it strives to be. Most importantly, that means the company has a culture people can identify with.

It is a fair rule of thumb to say that companies whose mission and vision are not easily recognizable, or don't strike an immediate chord, have not matched the words with their culture, which can create confusion when going through business transformation. People need something to connect to during the change.

Take part in the discussion at www.cheeky-monkey.co/connect

Cheeky Monkey Wisdom

There is a lot of discussion as to whether these statements have had their day and we should move towards charters in the same way Steve Jobs did with Apple. Whichever way you think suits you, there is no right or wrong: the information and intent is the same.

1 Google 2 Innocent 3 McDonalds 4 Amazon 5 Coca-Cola

Step 52

....

What is your business landscape?

Have a look at the next diagram, it illustrates how you can establish how your business does what it does. You can blow that up as big as you can get it and use sticky notes to put the answers on top. It should help you simplify what you do and get it all on one page.

Take part in the discussion at www.cheeky-monkey.co/connect

Cheeky Monkey Wisdom

Go back to basics with this. Think about the origins of the business: what has made it successful? What building blocks were put in place? Don't try and be too clever or overcomplicate it. You want the basic transactions that make your business make money.

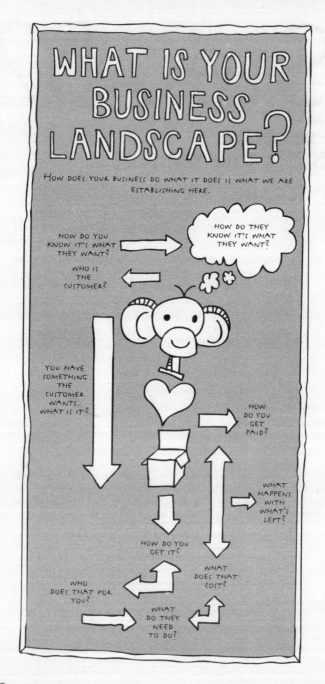

Step 53

Cheeky Monkey SWOT (Strengths, Weaknesses, Opportunities and Threats)

Still one of the best structures for a good old brain dump! You don't need to draw a matrix any more. Put all your thoughts down on sticky notes, one thought per note. Don't constrain your thinking trying to decide which box it's going to go in yet, just think about the following questions:

- What do you do better than anyone else?
- What could you improve?
- What should you avoid?
- What is your competition doing that you should be worried about?
- Is something changing that fundamentally affects your business?
- Do you have money worries?
- Do you know of something that could seriously damage your business?
- How do you get a sale now?
- Do you have (or access to) something unique?
- Why do you lose sales?
- What obstacles do you face?
- What are the interesting trends (technology, government policy, social behaviour, lifestyle, local events, people profile) you see happening around you?
- Where are the opportunities?
- Is technology threatening your position?
- What do other people see as your strengths?
- What do other people see as your weaknesses?

Take part in the discussion at www.cheeky-monkey.co/connect

Cheeky Monkey Wisdom

Don't over-analyse this. Go with your gut and get the ideas outside your head. Doing this as a group exercise is brilliant – the more diverse the group the better. All comments are valuable at this stage. And DON'T DISREGARD ANYTHING YET.

When you have run out of things to write, put your sticky notes up on the wall under the four headings: Strengths, Weaknesses, Opportunities and Threats. Be instinctive with this – go with your gut response and paste them up.

Step 54

Analysing strengths

When you have ideas under all four headings, take a step back and consider the following.

Think about what you have written in relation to your competitors. Put yourself outside your own world. If everyone has these strengths then they are essential just to stay in the game. Do you have anything over and above that? Think about people, innovation, design, sourcing, supplier partnerships, customer–consumer relationships, manufacturing processes, sales approach, ethics, ways of working, communication, brands, use of technology, delivery, after sales service, customer service and anything else I may have forgotten (you get my drift here).

Take part in the discussion at www.cheeky-monkey.co/connect

Cheeky Monkey Wisdom

Draw a circle around your special bits. If you haven't come up with any, put a ring around an empty space and write special bits inside it – do NOT let your heart sink at this early stage!

Step 55

Analysing weaknesses

Now depending on your personality type, this will be really easy or really hard. You have to think outside your own world again and be honest but realistic.

It can be easy some days to look at everything you do versus your competition and think you just don't cut it, you are there by luck and at some point someone will find out you are a fraud and your business will die.

On other days, you look at everything you do and think you are amazing, you have no idea why you aren't decimating your competition at every stage and believe there is nothing you need to change.

Take part in the discussion at www.cheeky-monkey.co/connect

Cheeky Monkey Wisdom

Face the unpleasant truths but try not to turn it into a self-harming session.

Step 56

Analysing threats

This is probably the easiest one to do because threats are real. Don't confuse threats with risks. Risks are things that may or may not happen. A threat is already happening or you know for a fact that it is coming.

Take part in the discussion at www.cheeky-monkey.co/connect

Step 57

Analysing opportunities

Think around different things that are happening externally and each function internally. Change is a huge opportunity so try and think about things that you know are changing. Look at your threats: are they really threats or are they actually opportunities? (Glass half full …) What about your weaknesses? Do they hold opportunities? If at first glance the answer to that is 'no', think harder so that they can!

Take part in the discussion at www.cheeky-monkey.co/connect

Cheeky Monkey Wisdom

Inspiration is a great source of opportunistic thinking. If you are struggling, search the web for your competitors and see what is being said about them. Look at the news on their websites. Look at websites of companies that you just love and see what they are up to. Search YouTube for video footage posted by prominent people (Boris Johnson is always good for a laugh, with a disturbing number of good points), look overseas at what is happening in India, China, Russia. The world is full of opportunity: don't restrict yourself and don't be constrained by a predetermined idea of what your business transformation is going to be. Under no circumstances say something is stupid, it could end up being the winning opportunity.

You might hit it first time, you may not, there is no right and wrong here. It is a dump of information which you have now categorized into four key areas of understanding. Don't take it down – we haven't finished yet.

Step 58

What do you do well?

You have a whole bunch of strengths on the wall (hopefully). Which of these are so fundamental to your business that you wouldn't outsource it/them? This is a lot tougher to answer than you think, because many of our best loved brands, owned by companies we know and cherish, don't make the products themselves anymore: complete supply chains have been outsourced through partnership agreements because other people can do that bit better/faster/ cheaper than the owner.

How far have you gone? More to the point – how far should you go? What are your core competencies?

Don't just look at your strengths, also look at your weaknesses. If you looked at outsourcing or using new technology to improve a weakness, could it become a core competency?

Look at the threats and opportunities: can you see something that if you could respond to it would become a core competency? Are you faced with something now, something you are missing out on because you can't respond, but you see a way that you can and then beat the competition?

Start making connections between those sticky notes focusing on:

▶ What do you do well now?
▶ What would you need to change to respond to an existing opportunity?
▶ What do you need to change to ensure a threat doesn't take you down?

Take part in the discussion at www.cheeky-monkey.co/connect

Cheeky Monkey Wisdom

Don't restrict yourself and start thinking about why you couldn't do those things. Things like money, time and expertise are not barriers yet.

Step 59

Business blueprint

We have the landscape you operate in, the market your products sit in, now we need to look at what's inside your business.

We need to create a business blueprint, a map of the systems, processes and people that allow you to do what you do.

As with the other maps, try and keep this as simple as possible. Don't go into too much detail (the following steps will guide you through that), otherwise you will tie yourself up in knots, get fed up and throw it away. At the point you feel frustrated, take it up a level.

When you get to activities, think:
- sourcing materials or goods
- forecasting demand (sales)
- production planning
- manufacturing
- quality
- distribution
- marketing
- sales
- customer service
- R&D
- new product development
- paying people (suppliers and employees)
- people paying you (customers and consumers)

When you get to processes and systems, think about:

- the technology that is being used
- forms and templates
- spreadsheets.

Take part in the discussion at www.cheeky-monkey.co/connect

BUSINESS BLUEPRINT

WHEN YOU GET TO PROCESSES AND SYSTEMS, THINK:
- ABOUT THE TECHNOLOGY THAT IS BEING USED
- FORMS AND TEMPLATES
- SPREADSHEETS

REVENUE GENERATING PRODUCTS AND SERVICES

MARKETS

SALES NUMBERS £'s

ALL THE ACTIVITIES REQUIRED TO DELIVER THE PRODUCTS AND SERVICES TO THE CONSUMER

FOR EACH ACTIVITY, THE SYSTEMS, PROCESS AND PEOPLE REQUIRED FOR DELIVERY

THE COST OF EACH ACTIVITY

Cheeky Monkey Wisdom

The blueprint is such a valuable document and it is worth investing some time in doing this and having the headspace to think about it. If you do, it will save you lots of time, pain and wasted resources further down the line. You don't have to be accurate with numbers but you do have to be close enough to be able to make the right judgements and decisions. The management team should be doing this together with the finance person responsible for chunking up the numbers.

Step 60

....

Cloud and the SAAS

Technology enables transformation. It has been a barrier to small companies because of the investment in the IT infrastructure required to make it all hang together, but not any more. Cloud computing is an IT delivery model based around the internet. It provides on-demand network access to a shared pool of computing resources: no need for networks, servers, storage, services or applications of your own and you can pay for what you need when you use it.

Software As A Service (SAAS) allows you to access software applications on a pay-as-you-go model. It's becoming more common and already extends into:

- accounting
- customer relationship management (CRM)
- enterprise resource planning (ERP)
- human resources management (HRM)
- collaborative applications, e.g. mail and calendars
- Product lifecycle management (PLM)

Your transformation will benefit from the introduction of technology but you must make sure that you look to join the dots. Understanding what you want to achieve and the processes and ways of working that already exist in the business is essential. SAAS is not customized or configured for you; therefore, the trade-off may be you have to change your ways of working or processes to get the alignment you need. Don't fall into the trap of believing that technology is the answer – it's just the enabler.

Take part in the discussion at www.cheeky-monkey.co/connect

Step 61

....

Stay fresh

It is so easy to get wrapped up in what we do day in, day out. Get up, sort the kids out maybe, work out (for the totally committed), get into the office; perhaps have the luxury of 30 minutes to an hour before you start the roll of meetings (physical and virtual), if you're lucky get a bit of 'work' done. Go home, do stuff, catch up on what you didn't get done during the day, fall into bed. Repeat.

Through those eyes the world can look quite small. How do you keep on top of what is going on in the world and in your area of interest? Welcome to social media. Twitter, Facebook, LinkedIn, blogs and forums open the world in a way that is efficient, engaging and can be done if you have five minutes or all day.

The whole idea is to engage, but if you are wary or shy of doing so straight away there is a mine of information you can investigate until you stumble across something that makes you want to engage.

Just in case you're a complete social media virgin, a quick summary of the main sites:

▶ **Facebook**. Yes the one where people put their 'status' and embarrassing pictures of themselves. It doesn't have to be that for you. You only have to be friends with people you want to be. There is a lot of content on Facebook.
▶ **LinkedIn**. Just for business networking. A chance to connect with people and catch up with what they are doing (and them you) and a wealth of discussion groups with people posting issues, interesting articles and stimulating debate.
▶ **Twitter** (my favourite). Just 140 characters to tell the world what you are doing. Best used as a vehicle to post links back to blogs or articles of interest. You can search on an area or person of interest

and see what people are saying. It's fast, concise and easy to navigate. Every day I read articles mentioned on Twitter that keep me in touch with what is going on; I would never find the time to do that via any other media.

▶ **Blogs and forums.** There are loads out there, and coming across anything of interest is trial and error. Good bloggers create content regularly and you can subscribe to regular feeds of those you like so the content drops directly into your email.

Take part in the discussion at www.cheeky-monkey.co/connect

Cheeky Monkey Wisdom

We use our websites as home. We blog and upload content that we want to share, and try and engage with people we know and welcome those we don't. We have automatic feeds that update LinkedIn and Facebook. Our friends on Facebook add to the content. We try and connect to everyone we have met on LinkedIn: it serves as our contact book and through our friends' contacts we have been introduced to some great people. We use Twitter to let people know we have things going on and when there is new content on our websites. We also use Twitter socially: our interests within Cheeky Monkey HQ are football, music and gaming, and we can be found discussing those things with the world at large.

Step 62

Where's the value?

Some things for you to do:

▶ On the blueprint, connect the activities together in the order that they happen.

▶ Circle the activities that have a direct relationship with creating what the customer wants. In that circle identify if it's delivering a question mark, star, cash cow or dog.

▶ Can you see how much effort and ultimately money is being attributed to each of these product (or service) groupings? Does that feel right when you look at the sales figures?

▶ Identify what links one activity to the next one. Is it a system, process or people?

▶ Grade (1 – weak, 2 – OK, 3 – great) the links between the activities. Does that feel right or are there opportunities to strengthen points of integration?

▶ Look at the opportunities you identified. Can you make them in this blueprint? If yes, show how. If no, identify the gaps.

Understanding value and eliminating waste are essential to business transformation. No matter how you dress them up if you just do those two things alone your business you will be more profitable and your growth will be sustainable.

Many companies don't take the time to look at how their system, processes and people link together. It is more usual that:

▶ There is a gap, or something that is not getting done, and they fill the gap, either with a system, process or person – the point at which all these areas link is usually clumsy and will result in people either using the system or process inefficiently or just not adopting it.

▶ They see an opportunity and plan to seize it without really understanding how that is going to affect everything else, and then fire-fight when problems start during execution.

Challenging the blueprint in this way should help you identify the areas of the business that require transformation to meet your business dream.

Take part in the discussion at www.cheeky-monkey.co/connect

Cheeky Monkey Wisdom

We know we shouldn't do things that don't add value, but some days you can't tell them apart from the things that do, so it's easier to continue to do them all. Some things we do are habit, some just historical and we've never really understood why. Things change and what once added real value could now just be noise. Practising lean working is like business transformation: it's a management principle that continues as the business grows and moves through its cycle of continuous improvement.

Step 63

Holistic sustainability

Holistic means looking at the whole to create the best outcomes. All our resources are in question, but every time someone tries to tell us the end is nigh, it isn't.

Our ability to innovate means that we avoid the world-ending moment, or so it seems. We deal with what we can see: there are always consequences and impacts somewhere, and when they surface we try and deal with them too.

Whether you believe that our resources are finite or not, you can't ignore that there are always consequences of our actions and we are becoming more aware of them. These things are having an impact on business structures, the way people view us and our businesses. You need to be conscious of them during your transformation; it doesn't mean you have to have people dedicated to sustainability (although if you are big enough having some internal warriors is never a bad thing); it's more important that all employees realize it is going to be part of your culture going forward and they all have their part to play.

Ten sustainable seeds you can plant:

1 Treat others with respect.
2 Give back to the community you operate in.
3 Minimize your carbon footprint as individuals and as a business.
4 Find out where the food you serve has come from and choose sustainable sources.
5 Think 'where has it come from?' before you buy anything.
6 Borrow before you get something new. (Do you really need it?)
7 Be careful with water.
8 Share transport.
9 Recycle.
10 Think globally but shop locally.

Cheeky Monkey Wisdom

Thinking about sustainability has a bonding effect because the easiest things to do involve human interaction: e.g. treating others with respect, sharing things instead of buying one for everyone, car pooling, giving back to the community. Some things are easier to do than others and there is no point in forcing things that add stress to people's lives, but making it a conscious and visible part of how you do business will make it the norm rather than an initiative that requires work.

Step 64

No customer, no business

On the chart you will have put down:

1 How you know it is what they want.
2 How do they know it's what they want?

This is about what you do today. We are working on business transformation, so you are looking to improve on that position. To improve we have to see the opportunities and discover the options.

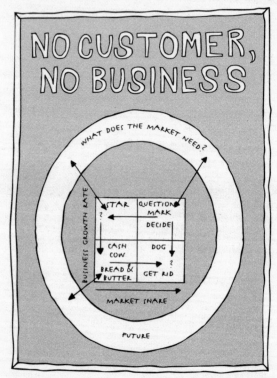

Again, you can blow this up and print it. It's a Boston Matrix in the middle; use sticky notes to plot your products and/or services according to their market share and business growth rate.

The circle around the outside the matrix is the future: what the market wants. Empty your head of everything you really know about what's going on in the world you operate in (and wider). You can add more circles if you think you need more structure to help your thinking. These prompts might help:

▶ Is there anything changing in your market place? e.g. new regulations
▶ Are changes in the political environment leading to discussions about your marketplace? e.g. import/export levies
▶ Environmental considerations, e.g. sustainable sourcing, recycling, carbon footprint.
▶ Impact of technology, e.g. demise of printed materials in favour of electronic reading devices.
▶ Social trends, e.g. more dads working from home and influencing traditionally female purchases.
▶ Global influences, e.g. politics, oil prices, economic cycles.
▶ Health and well-being, e.g. obesity.

Look at what you have in your Boston Matrix and see if you can match a future need with any of your products or services. Have you made a market discovery that will be so important to your marketplace that you need to develop a product or service? If you have, stick a big red ring around that.

Take part in the discussion at www.cheeky-monkey.co/connect

Cheeky Monkey Wisdom

You will feel some highs and lows going through this exercise and that may affect the people doing the exercise with you if they have been involved in things that haven't been as successful as you would have liked.
Don't waste energy being defensive or letting anyone else be defensive or feel like they have to explain. This is about looking forward – you are only looking back to move forward.

Step 65

···

Innovation is everywhere

In the same way that the elimination of waste from our supply chain has spread outside manufacturing and logistics into different types of the business, so has the concept of innovation.

Why leave the job of innovating within your business (the lifeblood of your business) to the technical development people and marketing teams when everyone can do it?

Whether you deliver products or services, the way your whole business synchronizes provides an experience that your customer receives. Encouraging innovation in every part of your business will generate untapped benefits.

This can be difficult to achieve with a workforce that is already doing more than the job descriptions state. In the spirit of open innovation, why not offer a profit-sharing initiative to financially reward the effort that may be required?

Take part in the discussion at www.cheeky-monkey.co/connect

Innovation checklist

Obvious	Not so obvious
R&D	HR
Product and service innovation	Business process
Sales	Distribution
Marketing	Sourcing
	Customer service
	Forecasting
	Manufacturing
	Quality
	Paying people
	People paying you

Cheeky Monkey Wisdom

During the start of the financial crisis, companies who
were hit by an immediate and unexpected downturn
turned to their employees and asked them what should
happen. Together the workforce found areas to innovate
and/or eliminate waste instead of resorting to redundancy
situations. In Julian's story (at the end of
section 2) he mentions how all the staff at the
hospital have come forward with a significant
sum of savings in support of the budget cuts
that have been forced on them.

Step 66

Finding unique

Obviously this is about the unique selling proposition (USP) of the business. Every business has one, you just have to find it –it might not be what you think it is.

Get the leadership team together for a couple of hours and brainstorm on finding unique. You'll need loads of sticky notes and pens, and a big sheet of paper on the wall.

Get everyone to brainstorm what it is your business does and the way that it does it; stick all the ideas on the wall.

When you have run out of steam, take a red pen and put a cross through everything that your competitors do too.

What are you left with?

It takes a few goes to get where you need to be with this because each time you compare yourself to your competition you will start to dig deeper and describe more about what you do versus what they do.

Keep posting up the sticky notes and using the red pen until you have the points that are unique to you.

Take part in the discussion at www.cheeky-monkey.co/connect

Cheeky Monkey Wisdom

We do live in 'me too' times and there is a chance that as you go through this exercise you think your points of difference are either too tenuous or just not relevant. As you compare yourself against your competition, you will start to home in on areas where you feel there should be a point of difference – as part of this transformation, you are going to make that happen.

Step 67

Mapping the lifecycle

Knowing what the lifecycles of your products and services are supports decision-making and prioritization. The simplest place to start is with a Boston Matrix.

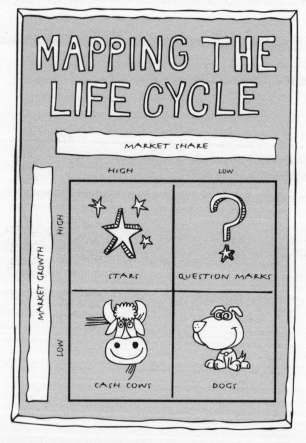

Stars. Stars are just that – they are doing well taking market share compared to their competition and are where your focus is right now. Probably still investing resources in support of them. (Action)

Cash cows. Where the money is coming from to support the more exciting business opportunities. Still generating revenue, but not taking too much investment, typically stars on the road to retirement. (Bread and butter)

Question marks. These are the ones that give you sleepless nights. They are teetering between brilliant and bin it, but you don't know which yet. (Decide)

Dogs. Low market share, low growth. You may have a brand-driven reason for keeping life support running but these aren't going anywhere and need to be monitored so they don't start leaking cash. (Get rid?)

Place your products and services in these boxes and see what you've got.

Take part in the discussion at www.cheeky-monkey.co/connect

Cheeky Monkey Wisdom

Make sure you are judging your products and services against your competition. It might be a star for your business, but is it in the market it trades in? There is not always the same match. Don't worry if you don't have products and services that are stars yet – that might be just your reason for transformation. Just be honest about where you are.

Step 68

Tuning into your customers

Questions that can keep the marketing community talking for hours:

1 How do you know what your customer wants?
2 Does your customer know what they want?
3 Where are they looking for what they want?
4 Who are they listening to?

There has of course been a social revolution in this area. People globally are shifting to the internet to either help with their decision-making process or buy online, or both. The shift towards people wanting to talk to other people is also marked; customers value another user's opinion, trusting it more than the advertising.

It's no wonder business has started to infiltrate this social world: customers seem to value it and that is where the money is. You need to figure out what your customers value and where they are going to get what they want.

Brainstorming is the most common tool for starting the ideas process and it's becoming increasingly complex:

▶ Do you think inside or outside the box?
▶ Are you stimulated by products that have gone before or products from a totally different sector? Or will silence enable the 'Aha' moment to be heard?
▶ Do you create clusters of people who are part of your core and on your rim?

Although I am in danger of seeming cynical about this step, it is important that you tune into your customers but also important that you know what you are going to get out of it:

- data? (easy)
- insights? (harder)
- ideas? (hard)
- the answer to what you do next? (really hard)

Connecting with your customers digitally seems the obvious and cost-effective route but the statistics show that we are getting fed up of this already. You need to make sure how you engage with your customer is relevant and wanted. It's like any relationship: both parties need to want it to happen in the first place and then keeping it going is hard work.

Five steps to tuning into your customer:

1 Understand who they are (age, gender, social background, likes and dislikes, etc.).
2 When you understand who your customers are, you also find out who your customers are not.
3 Find out how they like to talk (by invitation, through forums, via your website, anonymously, or they don't like to).
4 When you know how they like to talk, then you can ask them what makes them choose your product and services now (better, cheaper, available, lifestyle choice, brand loyalty, etc.).
5 When you have engaged and have a (two-way) relationship, your conversations can get wider and involve more participation, if that's what they are happy to do. Getting trusted customers involved in your innovation process is like having sunshine in your bag.

Take part in the discussion at www.cheeky-monkey.co/connect

Cheeky Monkey Wisdom

You are a customer, so are all the people who work in your business. This is a great way to start understanding how you should tune into your customers. Your customers are probably already talking about your products and services; search the usual outlets and see what they are saying (Twitter, Facebook and Google). Remember, no one wants to feel like they are being manipulated and used; treat people how you would want to be treated and you should have the basis for a long-lasting friendship.

Step 69

Doing what the customer wants

Having a product or service that your customer wants can start its journey from several different sources:

- ▶ customer insights
- ▶ trends in the marketplace
- ▶ new technology
- ▶ research and development.

These products and services fall into different categories:

- ▶ new product or service to new market
- ▶ new product or service to existing market
- ▶ existing product or service to new market
- ▶ existing product or service to existing market
- ▶ variation of product or service to new market
- ▶ variation of product or service to existing market.

Being clear about where your new products and services are coming from and going to helps to create a map of your journey and what kind of resource you are going to need to take that journey.

This is important because it is highly unlikely that you are going to be able to do all of them at the same time, so you need to be able to choose wisely.

The process in which you evaluate all the ways in which your business can do what the customer wants is not water-tight because at this stage you don't know everything. You need to be pragmatic and understand there are things that are just unknown at this stage; on top of that, things are full of risk, and may or may not happen.

Five steps to choosing how to do what the customer wants:

1 What is the reward for giving the customer what they want?
2 How does doing this align to what your business is looking to do, how it wants to be perceived and how it wants to grow?
3 What do you already have that contributes to giving the customer what they want with this product and/or service in this market?
4 Be the bookmaker: what odds do you give yourself of being able to succeed commercially in the market?
5 Now give yourself odds for being able to deliver the product or service to the market in time to take the opportunity: what are they?

Take part in the discussion at www.cheeky-monkey.co/connect

Cheeky Monkey Wisdom

Getting into the rhythm of establishing what your customers want, mapping that to your own grading process and choosing where to focus your resources is the equivalent of creating the business heartbeat. Innovation is the lifeblood of all businesses; people, process, technology, the heart; how you choose and deliver what your customer wants, the heartbeat. You are obviously looking for constant, not irregular!

Step 70

You are not alone

Creating connections can help your business transformation in so many ways; open innovation is a perfect one to start with if you are not already there.

The concept was put on paper by Henry Chesbrough back in 2003, yet it still feels like it's in its infancy. At its simplest form, open innovation is about people working together (inside and outside your business) throughout the innovation process. The concept is that you can be better together and there are several ways to do this:

▶ Work with external research and development companies.
▶ Partner with inventors and entrepreneurs.
▶ Buy intellectual property.
▶ Sell intellectual property.
▶ Co-create with your customers.

Why do this? Why open your doors? Because you have to kiss a lot of frogs before you find your prince!

There are different levels to consider here. Many companies don't really innovate. When you consider the vast proportion of product innovation comes from packaging design or me too introductions and a variation on a theme that is already out there, real innovation is rare.

The service sector suffers from the same. When you are delivering a service you differentiate in the customer experience. Creating a genuinely new customer experience is equally challenging and then there are the services that products deliver.

Henry has more recently written about being conscious of the customer experience attached to product use; understanding this has already led to creative market propositions in on-demand car hire, and the opportunity to design your own clothes and shoes and then buy them.

Bringing this back to you and your business: how far are you going to survive taking into account the challenges in Step 1 without learning the art of kissing?

A table for you to consider:

Open innovation route	What you could achieve
Meeting with the people who supply you to discuss reward-sharing opportunities for the introduction of new ideas that could be commercialized	Unmet market needs. Two, three ... ten heads are better than one
Creating cluster groups in different geographic locations combining start-up businesses, entrepreneurs and suppliers who have knowledge and experience of new markets	Extending your business into a new or emerging space. This can be a case of copy and paste if you have the right connections and knowledge
Sponsoring or becoming part of a business incubator. Aligning with academic institutions and research foundations who are looking for and developing future breakthroughs	Being part of the future. This type of innovation still has a huge failure rate; private enterprise funding research (which the public sector can't afford) has got to be a winning combination

Take part in the discussion at www.cheeky-monkey.co/connect

Cheeky Monkey Wisdom

Open innovation is about trust, being competitive without being adversarial, and looking at the long-term gains in addition to the short-term wins. Globalization and sustainability are forcing open innovation deeper into organizations now. The digital age is also making open innovation easier. There is no excuse for not having this as part of your business transformation.

Step 71

Working in the global village

There is a chance that the people you need to work with routinely are not in the same office or even country as you. Having your workforce scattered around different time zones from different backgrounds, cultures and speaking a different language provides a cosmopolitan set of challenges.

The biggest one is communication. In our virtual world you don't get face time, adding to the importance of understanding how you sound when you talk.

This is so important you need to record yourself. You will be able to do it on a smart phone. Take this seriously as it will make a huge difference to your work.

Use some material that is real. If you have a meeting coming up that you are going to lead, brilliant, use that. Record yourself talking as you would in your meeting. Play it back. What do you hear?

CHECKLIST:

► Do you sound interesting?
► Do you sound interested in what you are doing?
► Can you understand what you are saying? Does it make sense?
► Are you concise? Or do you waffle?
► Is there a clear point to what you are saying?
► Is your use of language easy to understand?
► Can you hear different emotions?
► Do you talk too fast or too slowly?
► Do you have any annoying habits, e.g. saying 'like' or 'urm' a lot?
► If English isn't your first language, can you and others understand what you are saying?

It is hard to do this because we all hate hearing the sound of our own voices but talking is an art form and you can learn how to talk effectively so that people listen and understand. Be honest with yourself: are you good or is this an area where you could use help?

The way in which you structure meetings also makes a difference to what you get out of them. It's not only the spoken word that needs to be simple and clear, the written word does too.

When you are writing, make sure it is unambiguous and be very clear about what you want to happen, especially if you are expecting someone else to do it.

Some virtual meeting basics:

▶ Send the agenda ahead of time and make sure all participants understand what is expected of them before the meeting.
▶ Take it in turns to be the early morning or late night participant and acknowledge that with those that are doing it (just say thanks).
▶ Establish some meetings norms; e.g. always start talking introducing your name first (of course until you know each other), don't talk over each other, allow time for people to respond (they might be translating what you are saying).
▶ Make sure everyone is involved. Some cultures will hold back – use questions to get them to respond so that you can check understanding.
▶ Use a mixture of tools and create meeting notes while the meeting is going so that people can follow what is being agreed; this will stop misunderstandings after the meeting.
▶ Avoid long discussions that don't involve everyone; take specifics into follow-up calls.
▶ Use examples to illustrate what you are saying to make sure the essence of what you are talking about is understood if the literal translation is not enough.
▶ Have some fun. Meetings can be stressful and people need to feel at ease, able to ask for clarifications and make mistakes.

Take part in the discussion at www.cheeky-monkey.co/connect

Cheeky Monkey Wisdom

Even though I have worked with global virtual teams for over five years, it still takes discipline. You want your personality to come across so that relationships are made but you have to recognize the need for simplicity. Despite the amazing technology that exists, nothing is as good as spending time with people face to face; once that relationship exists then remote working is easy. For long-term significant transformation projects, I still try and get the organization to agree to at least a kick-off meeting for everyone involved – it's not a jolly, it's about creating a connection.

Step 72

The order of events

Previous steps might have left you with a list as long as your arm or a nice logical concise programme that makes perfect sense. Either way, it is unlikely that you have the resources to do everything you want at the same time. It makes sense at this point to start the translation of what you need to do into action and give it some order.

This should help you see what can be done with little fuss and disruption, what you should stop doing and what is going to form one or more projects. The projects will probably underpin your business transformation and form the basis of the communication you provide to the business. Make sure you take the opportunity to talk about the 'no-brainers' and the 'gap fillers' so that everyone understands the whole situation has been reviewed and small, but probably annoying, actions are going to get done.

Take part in the discussion at www.cheeky-monkey.co/connect

Cheeky Monkey Wisdom

Taking into account the small annoying stuff while you are deciding on business transformation priorities is really appreciated by the people who, day to day, have to deal with the small annoying stuff that always seems to get overlooked in favour of a bigger more exciting project. This will show everyone you mean business; it's been thought and worked through.

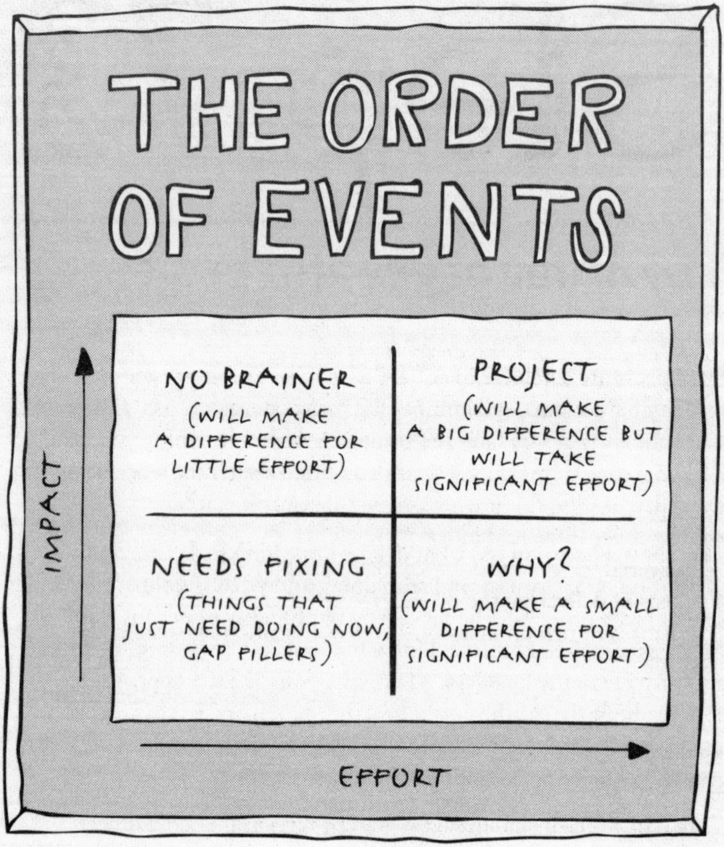
THE ORDER OF EVENTS
NO BRAINER
(WILL MAKE A DIFFERENCE FOR LITTLE EFFORT)
PROJECT
(WILL MAKE A BIG DIFFERENCE BUT WILL TAKE SIGNIFICANT EFFORT)
NEEDS FIXING
(THINGS THAT JUST NEED DOING NOW, GAP FILLERS)
WHY?
(WILL MAKE A SMALL DIFFERENCE FOR SIGNIFICANT EFFORT)
IMPACT
EFFORT

Step 73

Project management basics

- Projects are a vehicle to deliver change to the business.
- They have a start and end date.
- At the end they will deliver something tangible.
- The scope of the project needs to align clearly with a business goal.
- Resources (time and money) are allocated against the tasks to be delivered.
- Costs of delivering the project are detailed, as well as the business return on investment requirement on delivery of the project.
- Projects are planned in advance of work starting and that plan (or definition document) agreed with stakeholders prior to starting.
- The plan (widest sense) or project definition document is the baseline for all changes to be mapped against.
- Issues, risks and changes are kept in controlled documents and any significant impact mapped back to the definition document.
- Regular meetings are held:
  - with a business group of people who need this to happen (steering group)
  - for the project team led by the project manager
- Projects end with a review of tangible delivery against objectives, and a review of the effectiveness of the team and way of working that can feed into the next project.

Take part in the discussion at www.cheeky-monkey.co/connect

Cheeky Monkey Wisdom

There is a growing project culture in most businesses now, but many are still done in addition to people's day jobs, using people who have little experience or understanding of how to run projects. If this is the case, get them some support, it's worth the investment and it's a skill set you will need continually as you strive for further improvements.

Step 74

Choosing a programme manager

In my view, there are people who are qualified to do these roles and those who can naturally do these roles. In the case of a programme manager, you need someone who is experienced enough to do this role.

If you look around for a programme manager the chances are they will have come out of the IT world; programme managers with a breadth of business experience are hard to find and you need to look beyond the job title for this role. Don't think 'programme manager', think what is the final outcome I am looking for and does this person have the experience to guide us there?

Then think about the people this person will be working with – your project managers – what are they like? Is there going to be harmony, sparks or fireworks? People don't have to like each other to work together, but there does have to be an element of matching even if it is just professional respect.

The programme manager is not looking to deliver the project but instead will ensure that the related projects deliver the outcome. This is less storm trooper, more master manipulator (in the most positive sense). This person doesn't need the glory, is already confident and self-assured, knows how to navigate a path to success regardless of what is thrown at them, and is one of the most organized and methodical people you know.

And you must trust their judgement; otherwise, you will end up doing their job.

Take part in the discussion at www.cheeky-monkey.co/connect

Step 75

Choosing a project manager

There are qualified project managers and people who have been
told by their boss they are going to manage a project as an addition
to their day-to-day job (I see this all the time). Managing projects
requires a skill set (planning, objective setting, budget control, risk
and issue management, communication and people management) like
all other jobs and a set of personality traits that are, in my view, more
important than the skill set. In this case, there is no need to have one
without the other.

The project manager is the one who is going to deliver specifically
what you have asked for using the resources you have allocated to
them and within a timeframe you have agreed. If they haven't got
the skill set to do that, it will cost you more than the price of some
training in project over-runs and failures. Wise up: don't put your
transformation deliverables into the hands of people who don't have
the tools to do the job!

And you want them to have the energy and agility of Super Mario
because it's infectious and priceless.

Project managers do not have to have technical experience or
knowledge of the project (it's a bonus if they do) they are going to
manage because that will exist in the team – the team members bring
that from their respective functions – but they need to be able to get
a team to deliver for them when they will not be their line managers
(no authority).

Our top ten things a great project manager should be:

1 Seen as a leader
2 Able to win the hearts and minds of the team
3 Enthusiastic and have a general lust for life
4 Happy when all is not clear
5 Able to juggle business priorities
6 Confident about how and when to say NO
7 Able to keep everyone working when things are going wrong
8 Dependable so people know they can rely on you
9 A trampoline for information (see, digest, act)
10 A decision-maker

Take part in the discussion at www.cheeky-monkey.co/connect

Cheeky Monkey Wisdom

All Cheeky Monkey project managers are Prince2 practitioners. We don't run projects using the Prince2 methodology, but it is a sound foundation to teach them The Way of the Monkey and provides a baseline from which to grow and experience the causes and effects of different elements of project delivery. You can do these courses in a week; if this is new to everyone it's worth the investment.

If you can't find someone who ticks all the boxes, then in this case go for personality and personality traits over experience. A project manager with no drive may as well be an empty chair.

When asked, my fellow Monkeys said the most important attribute of our Project Managers was a natural smile ☺

Step 76

Choosing project team members

On paper these are the easy people to pick: they are the people who are already working in your business who will be bringing the required expertise and experience to the project. The big issue here is always: do they have the time to do it?

I am not a fan of herding lots of consultants onto a client site to deliver projects; it's not sustainable and it's soul-destroying for the people who work for you to be on the receiving end of change and not able to influence and shape what is going to happen. Neither, though, am I a fan of lazy managers who do not take the time to resource-plan, prioritize and make decisions to allow their staff the headspace to be involved in delivering projects.

Take part in the discussion at www.cheeky-monkey.co/connect

Cheeky Monkey Wisdom

Who makes up the project team should be a no-brainer but it is so often an uncomfortable time because the leaders know who they want but feel they can't release them from what they are already doing or they are already working on too many projects. Finding a way of sharing experience and knowledge in the business has to become a priority during business transformation: key employees can't be a bottleneck and other employees need to rise to the challenge or go.

Step 77

Resource planning

So you have to resource-plan first. This has got to be one of the most over-complicated tasks I see (on the rare occasions I actually see it). Seriously . . .

We don't need to get to timesheets and counting hours at this stage, you will know if the right people are available to work on your projects at the right time with something as basic as this. Be conscious that this is happening in addition to business as usual, so you may need help either in the business or in the project. That help should be included in the budget so that a clear return on that investment can be delivered.

Thinking about the mix of people in project teams is important, not from the perspective of personality fit (although it does make life easier), but more importantly what is their social status in the business? Are they the voices of doom any time anything changes? Are they the office mums always looking out for everyone? Party organizers? Unofficial fix-it people? Thought leaders? Sheep?

These unofficial roles that people have in the work environment are brilliant to tap into when you are delivering change; they already have a network and love to use it and you just can't buy that. Try and spread them around. Same goes for the naysayers, those voices of doom need to be inside and not out (unless they are really bad then they should just be on their way out). There is nothing more powerful than hearing the voices of doom start chirping about how it's not that bad after all.

Take part in the discussion at www.cheeky-monkey.co/connect

Cheeky Monkey Wisdom

Choice, decisions and consequences . . . don't stick your head in the ground and hope that the individual's personal pride and ability to work 24/7 will win the day again. Eventually, those great people that you value so much and put on every project will get fed up and leave.

Look at everyone you have to choose from. When I go into businesses, I always find at least one gem who has been undiscovered. Look beyond your usual hot picks, and they might surprise you.

People cost money. In the same way you would do a return on investment proposal for a piece of equipment, if resource is short, do it to build a case for people. Projects fail because there just wasn't enough resource to do what needed to be done despite people's best efforts. Calculate the cost of failure and the lost opportunity cost of not doing something.

Resource planning should also be done as part of the project definition document where the project Gantt chart should show you where there are resource demand peaks.

Step 78

The project definition document

This question and answer checklist clarifies what you are trying to
achieve with this document.

Question	The answer will give you
Why are we doing this?	The purpose of the project and its results
What are we being asked to deliver?	Scope of the project
How are we going to deliver it?	Approach
How are we going to measure our success?	Objectives
How will we meet customer expectations?	Customer acceptance criteria/critical success factors (if we don't do these, we kill the project)
How much will it cost?	Budget
What is the expected return on investment?	Forecast
Who needs to be involved?	Roles and responsibilities
When do we need to deliver it?	Timeline
What controls are in place to manage change?	Issue and change control process
What obstacles might stop us?	Risk management process
Can we win with this?	Looking back at everything – what do the team think?

Keep the document simple but complete. The document should be a team effort and is best completed during a project kick-off meeting. This meeting should be high energy and interactive, and should provide the perfect opportunity to set the tone for the project. So when the project team is asked 'can we win with this?' there is air-punching and dancing (if you work in Nigeria this is what happens) – complete commitment to the cause.

Take part in the discussion at www.cheeky-monkey.co/connect

Cheeky Monkey Wisdom

This one document can be the difference between project success and failure (and definitely the difference between happy project teams and frustrated ones).

Step 79

···

The ingredients for a great project kick-off workshop

▶ one facilitator who cares about more than themselves (ideally the project manager but not essential – sometimes an external facilitator can really help)
▶ a recap of the presentation on the business transformation delivered by a big fish
▶ lots of dots to show the connection between the proposed initiatives, those already running and this one (up on the wall so people can refer to it)
▶ the timeline this project has to fit into and why (delivered by the programme manager, if there is one)
▶ the people who are going to work on the project (all of them – no exceptions)
▶ loads of paper, pens and sticky notes (still can't be beaten for this kind of session)
▶ coffee, green tea, nice biscuits and good sarnies (the sort of stuff that visitors usually get)
▶ eggs, card, straws, balloons, paper and tape (for 'defend the egg' (Step 80), a great afternoon energizer)
▶ lots of creative materials if you are going down the creative route so you can make treasure maps and the project quilt (and a camera)

Agenda for the day

The intention of the day is to complete a project definition document, the content of which we have gone through. Depending on the background of the team, you may choose to make this a more creative playful session or keep it straight and to the point. Doing these in several countries around the world, my experience is: UK and Australia, keep it straight; Asia and Africa, make it as creative as you can.

Straight	Creative
Scope Objectives Deliverables	What the boss wants Single version of the truth Our promise
Approach What needs to happen to deliver the project	**Treasure map** Create the route from where we are now to where we need to be
Project timeline Breakdown objectives Create work breakdown structure Assign work packages Agree dependencies Map overall timeline	**Project quilt (friendship exercise)** All the squares that need to come together to deliver the objectives Agreement on how they get stitched together Who is doing what and when
Critical success factors Things that are so critical to the success of the project if they didn't happen we would kill the project	**The emergency cord (recognition and alerting exercise)** Things that are so critical to the success of the project if they didn't happen we would kill the project
Risk brainstorm Everything that could happen How likely is it How will we manage it	**What might stop us?** Everything that could happen How likely is it How will we manage it

Issue collection	What is stopping us now?
Things we already know are going to hit us	Things we already know are going to hit us
How we are going to get over them	How we are going to get over them
Who is going to take care of it	Who is going to take care of it

Meeting and reporting schedule	Talking and getting together (make it social)
How (physical and virtual)	How (physical and virtual)
How often	How often
What's expected	What's expected

Take part in the discussion at www.cheeky-monkey.co/connect

Cheeky Monkey Wisdom

Project kick-off workshops should be amazing energy days where the project team come together, perhaps for the first time, to agree how they are going to ace this business request. These should be cross-functional teams and, as with the steering group, business status and hierarchy doesn't transfer into the project – you are there as the best team to do the job. Team, trust and confidence building have to happen all day, so that you can work remotely when the project definition has been agreed. Working on projects should be fun and an opportunity to experience things outside business as usual; work hard on that and the team will respond.

Step 80

Defend the Egg energizer

Defend the Egg (also known as the Great Egg Drop) is a high energy, very competitive team-building game that involves collaboration, problem-solving, and creative teamwork.

The idea is simple: you go somewhere high (roof garden of a hotel, stairwell, stand on a table, whatever you can do to create height) and drop a raw egg straight on the floor. It smashes (it makes a mess so prepare for that), everyone gasps that you have really just done that – then tell the groups they have to build a structure out of the materials in the room to try to protect their raw egg from breaking when dropped from the same point. You must be able to see the egg at all times, otherwise you will get eggs packed in boxes (your projects teams are not idiots).

This exercise in team-building is messy, so choose an appropriate setting where making a mess is acceptable. (I have had to apologize so many times for doing this but it's always worth it!)

Give them about 20 minutes to defend their egg.

Hype up the egg dropping and after each one carefully inspect to see if the eggs survived. The winners are the groups that successfully protected their eggs.

Take part in the discussion at www.cheeky-monkey.co/connect

Cheeky Monkey Wisdom

If you are doing this in a hotel, make sure that all normal hotel guests are out of the way or you may be asked to leave by the hotel management (or so I've heard ...)

STORY 6: FAMILY VALUES

Storytellers: Iain Speak and Paul Byrne

Bibby Distribution is part of the Bibby Line Group, a diversified family-owned business based in Liverpool and founded in 1807. What is unusual about Bibby is that its shares remain in the control of the direct descendents of the original founder, and this translates into over 200 years experience of embracing change and of refining a formula that creates long-term growth.

Today, the Group generates annual revenues in excess of £1 billion, and operates substantially autonomous trading businesses in the financial services, convenience retail, marine, logistics and offshore oil and gas sectors.

Bibby Distribution is among the UK's top ten logistics providers, and is a growing and increasingly influential player in the UK contract logistics sector. In pursuit of its growth strategy, Bibby completed five successful acquisitions in 2010.

Me: In 1993 I wrote in a university paper on supply chain management saying that transport as it was known then was about to transform into distribution and logistics. Transport companies were just starting to realize that they could offer a complete solution to their clients which integrated them fully into the supply chain. In the history of Bibby, when did that transformation start happening? When did you stop being just about transport and start being about solutions?

Iain: Probably about 1993, although with hindsight we have always looked to provide our customers with solutions, the significant change has been how we market and sell those solutions today.

Me: Transformation for you is about giving the customer what they want?

Iain: It's about being proactive about that, changing what we do so that we can go to our customers with ideas and initiatives. That could be anything from a relatively small continuous improvement project to something very big. We can do things that our customers can't, especially with integration of activities in the value chain. Our customers have silos and we have networks; they can benefit from the way we operate and we can deliver tangible savings.

Me: Does every transformation deliver a benefit?

Iain: We are always looking to deliver benefits but we are also aware that we are not in control of everything. Things happen that result in transformation being imposed on you and it's not always positive. We try to be proactive with these too by managing the risks that we think we have in the business, these are so important to us that they are allocated to each board member.

Me: The way that you transform within this group is not only by looking directly at transport and logistics as a business, it's by integrating associated companies. Is that part of risk management?

Paul: What you mean in terms of investing in different types of activity, do we do it to lessen risk? No.

Me: Why do you do it?

Iain: To maximize opportunity.

Paul: We do it to drive growth.

Me: From the little experience I've had, you are really quite structured about the way that you take over a company and the way that it's integrated, and the focus is surprisingly soft. What is the strategy behind how you integrate these associated companies?

Paul: The value inherent in those activities that we invest in is largely in the people that exist within them, and so we have to create an environment in which they'll continue to deliver that value because we can't because that's not the game we're in. That's the basic premise.

Iain: For over 200 years our Group has been about embracing change. More recently, we have created an infrastructure, a management competency and a value set that is about continuous improvement which has created a solid foundation for growth. Transport is a low-margin business (about 3 per cent) so if we do more of the same we will grow but our margin will stay the same.

Our view is we can understand what we are good at and use that strength to invest in other activities, markets that have completely different economic characteristics and have the potential to grow our margin as well as our revenues.

Paul: And our people-focused approach comes back to a Group philosophy that's around creating an infrastructure and environment where you can make decisions as close to the action as possible, as close to the customer as possible. Which obviously gives you the ability to tailor and bespoke your service where it delivers most value, but it requires the individuals and the management of the people concerned to have the ability and the confidence to make those calls within that infrastructure. So the soft approach is enabling the people to create an environment where they can make decisions for themselves, not the other way round.

Me: Your approach focuses on sustainability because you do put a lot of energy and investment into making the people who are there already become more of an asset, helping them grow faster giving them the support to do it.

Iain: Absolutely, but it's because we believe it to be the right way to develop our business – if they are better, we are better.

Me: Many organizations would just go for the quick win, parachute somebody else in, and what you do is very different to that.

Paul: It's about understanding where the value is, and quite often corporate businesses that acquire other businesses will be driven to make large cost savings immediately because that's how they price the deal. The deal assumes that the head office is going to be taken out on day five and so they do what they have to do to get the deal done, and then it forces them to act in a way that probably actually erodes lots of the value that was the reason they bought the business in the first place.

So we don't do that, which means we don't pay as much because we think we have a formula that will enable us to maintain and build upon the inherent value that lies in the business. And nothing about it is easy, and neither does it mean that we are soft on making the right decisions about how you drive efficiency. But it's with an agenda to grow the businesses and to grow the people.

Me: So does your private status give everybody here a level of confidence that it doesn't matter what everyone else thinks?

Paul: Well it doesn't. As a private family-owned business we have a different set of stakeholders, we are not looking to demonstrate an enhanced earnings per share on a quarterly basis, we are there to provide long-term growth for a set of family shareholders and because of the values that those shareholders hold, we have to do that in a way that is consistent with the way that they see the world, so it does drive a certain type of behaviour.

We have the same pressures though, we have the performance pressures. You wouldn't be here if the numbers of the business were consistently going backwards.

Me: The next ten years for Bibby and Bibby Distribution, where's your focus?

Paul: Long-term sustainable profit.

Iain: Agree.

Me: How?

Paul: By responding to the opportunities that will inevitably present themselves.

Iain: By preparing ourselves to be ready for those opportunities. It's about getting our people to manage up instead of historically what's happened, and still does in most other companies, where people manage down. We want everybody to manage up because that's going to create headroom and growth, or headroom in line with the growth.

Me: What do you mean by managing up?

Iain: Push boundaries; feel able to take calculated risks.

Paul: Take ownership.

Iain: Be responsible at every level, be aware of the consequences of their actions, be aware of themselves, be aware of how they're perceived by others around them. Think outside of the box, to push themselves to the boundary, their boundary, we aren't going to define it. If they do that it's going to create capacity. That capacity hopefully will be in line with the growth that we've got planned. It will then create opportunities and we'll be able to satisfy internal aspiration and ambition.

Me: In everything that you talk about and have talked about today, for you it's all about the people.

Iain: If we can be the best employer of people we'll be the most efficient, we'll get the most discretionary effort, we'll have the lowest sick and absence rates, we'll have the lowest staff turnover, when we need people to go that extra mile they will, they'll enjoy it. In return we'll give them a career and security.

Me: What's your definition on transformation?

Paul: I don't know if I've got one. What's my definition of transformation? Transformation is significant change. It can be positive or negative. In the business context we are looking for transformation because we're looking to change the dynamics of how we do things to improve them. That's probably it.

Section 7
Magic

CREATIVITY

Step 81

....

Love

We are at a crossroads. We want more from our working lives than money (for most people that has always been the case) and the world has changed to a point where this is now a choice many people can make (which has not always been the case). Step 1 describes the move to flatter, more networked organizations; this is not just driven by the corporate world, it's because we want more out of our working lives and if the corporate world won't deliver it, we will find another way. Not all the smart people want to work for you anymore.

If you skipped to this step looking for a bit of sex and romance, you are going to be disappointed but don't stop reading. It's about the need for move love and care about what we do in the workplace because it has a far-reaching effect on things that are important:

▶ people (compassion and consideration for)
▶ making decisions that affect the world we live in.

In Step 48, we talk about left and right brain thinking; this is definitely right brain. We have been through a period of cold logic and dispassionate decision-making that has been primarily focused on delivering cold hard cash and shareholder value. I'm not suggesting love is going to replace that, but the balance needs to be addressed during transformation.

Let's consider the facts:

▶ increase in people wanting to be part of a co-operative or employee ownership scheme, e.g. John Lewis model

- jump in demand for 'fair trade' products and the belief in what that stands for
- growing contempt for big bonus payouts for business leaders when their staff struggle with wage freezes and constant redundancy warnings.
- awareness of the global community, how corporate decisions translate into products we buy that then affect how people in different parts of the world live.

We want to see:

- people acting more responsibly
- caring for people and the planet
- a sense of right and wrong.

We want more love in the working world.

If you are a clinical leader then this transition is going to be tough but the rewards will be massive. For most leaders it's about awareness first, then action.

Bringing love into the workplace basics:

- Create plans that include people and their beliefs and point of view.
- Be responsible with decision-making, understand the implications on people and the environment, and act with compassion as well as logic and competitive drive.
- Have an ethical guide that displays a good sense of right and wrong to help with distributed decision-making.
- Put yourself out there and show you care. Be the first to say hello, be friendly, talk about emotions, smile, trust your instincts and believe that your actions can change the world. It's very contagious and will attract a following.

Take part in the discussion at www.cheeky-monkey.co/connect

Cheeky Monkey Wisdom

Cheeky Monkey is a self-filtering process. For a time we advertised it as being 'only for the enlightened' as we knew that we wouldn't want to work with the people who didn't get it. Our approach is based on the love of people and the belief we can change the world and we do. We don't chase money first but believe if you do the right things in the right way it will follow and thankfully it does. We are competitive and tough business architects who deliver multi-million pound transformations all over the world: it's not fluff, it is sustainable and it makes sense.

Step 82

Body language

It is said that the body is capable of making 700,000 movements. If you search the internet for 'body language expert', there are just short of 10 million results. This is a big subject.

It seems since psychologists have been able to understand what we say through our movements and gestures we have been hooked. Not surprisingly, if you are aware of body language, your own and someone else's, you are at an advantage. It's not about what they are saying, it's what they are not saying that is always more interesting.

Being aware is where it's at, as the nurture versus nature debate confirms. Some body language is involuntary and instinctive; these are usually small movements in the eyes and around the mouth. Others come through conditioning and because we learn them. These vary depending on cultural background.

Charles Darwin came up with the basics when he said that there were six facial expression recognized around the world:

- ▶ happiness
- ▶ sadness
- ▶ fear
- ▶ disgust
- ▶ surprise
- ▶ anger.

These six things tie into the basic human emotions and are genetically inherited, not dependent on social conditioning or learning and are the same everywhere – amazing. So it doesn't matter if you are leading a team of people from the different counties of the UK or representatives from each of the continents in the world, you can share the basic human emotions.

In my experience, the most useful interpretation of body language, after emotion, is to tell you when people are bored. When time is so precious, you need to make sure that you have the attention of everyone and people are usually too polite to tell you when you have lost them. You need to know that so that you can do something about it, otherwise people will avoid coming to your meetings.

You know when people are bored when they:

▶ don't look at you when they are talking
▶ doodle
▶ stare around the room
▶ look at their watch
▶ move with constant repetition (tapping fingers, swinging feet, playing with tie, etc.)
▶ yawn
▶ slouch in their seat or against the wall
▶ have a blank facial expression.

Body language is not a science and is open to interpretation so tread carefully, but sometimes just asking someone outright if you are boring them is enough for those indicators listed above to change or for that person to confess to being out all night. As you build a relationship with the people you are working with, encourage them to tell you if what you have invited them to is of no use to them or if the way you are explaining it is not engaging enough.

Going through transformation is tough and there will be lots of times when you need to see the signs of emotion and/or boredom: process it and take some action to keep everyone motivated. Look for what they are not telling you and face them with it.

Take part in the discussion at www.cheeky-monkey.co/connect

Cheeky Monkey Wisdom

You need a bit of body armour for this as understanding people's body language is as much about you facing how people react to your actions as much as it is them acknowledging that behaviour and it can feel very personal. Stay positive about this: it's all about learning and development. If you know what it is you do and how that is interpreted, you can change it or learn how to use it.

Step 83

Smile

Smile. It increases your face value.

Anonymous

Do it now. What happens? Your eyes automatically open wider. Your face wakes up, feels like it's alive. Your brain switches gear. It's like turning the ignition key on a car; you start to feel like you are ready to do something.

What happens to the people watching you? If you don't normally smile they will ask 'what are you up to?' (which is fun). If you smile a lot they will naturally smile back at you. Either way you have just flicked the ignition switch on someone else and a smile was all it took to engage with them.

For those of you who require science to believe anything:

▸ It takes 17 faces muscles to smile and 43 to frown.
▸ You release endorphins, natural painkillers and serotonin – happy drugs.
▸ Smiling relieves stress, boosts your immune system and lowers blood pressure.
▸ It makes you look younger.

Peace begins with a smile.

Mother Teresa

Mother Teresa was so right: smiling makes people feel warm, safe and trusting – the basis for breaking down barriers and starting great relationships.

My smiling comes from the fact I love life (and perhaps a touch of madness). I love what I do and do what I love, and I know that's not the same for everyone. There will be things that you love, that make you smile every time you think about them. So spend more time thinking about them than the stuff that doesn't make you smile. It sounds easy because it is.

Business transformation is about relationships at every level. Smiling will not only make you feel better, it will make you look better and your life easier.

When you smile, the whole world smiles with you … it's so true.

Take part in the discussion at www.cheeky-monkey.co/connect

Cheeky Monkey Wisdom

Cheeky Monkey was designed to make people smile first before we did anything, even speak. We believe in a human approach to innovation and change. Human interaction is what we focus on. Smiling is so simple, it's a perfect start.

Step 84

It is about you

Being a leader means that in some situations and on some days you stand alone. You ultimately carry the responsibility, the buck stops with you, good or bad. You might be responsible for people's jobs, promotions and futures within the business.

There will be times when you are lost but can't tell anyone or show it to your team, knowing that there is nothing left to do but wait without panicking. This takes courage and is stressful.

You need to make sure you look after yourself first. This isn't a selfish gesture, it's about making sure you are OK to look after everyone else.

Be aware of your own limits, triggers and touch points. You are only human and sometimes you are going to have a bad day and the chances are others will feel it. If you know it's happening, you can diffuse the situation and also relieve some tension by sharing it and laughing about it.

Leaders need support structures. If you have the backing of a clear decision-making process, this will be a huge support. You need to know who is there to underpin the painful or complex decisions, and allow you to check decisions that have to be made when things are uncertain. Remember that no matter how important you are, you still play only a part in a much larger picture.

Finding a mentor is a real bonus. A trusted mentor can be that sounding board where you test and develop your thinking. They can also be the reality check you will need when you are going down the wrong rabbit hole and need someone to shine a light on the way out.

All work and no play makes you boring and narrow-minded. You need to experience life to lead people, and finding the time and space to do that is as important as the work. You are also the example people will either follow or get stressed about because they can't follow.

Take part in the discussion at www.cheeky-monkey.co/connect

Cheeky Monkey Wisdom

I am a workaholic: I admitted that a long time ago, but I have a lust for life that is at least equal for my love of work. The way I live my life would not suit everyone – my work and life are welded together in so many fundamental ways, but it enables me to do all the things I want, and keeps me happy, fresh and with loads to share with the people I work with. No one wants to be led by a person who has nothing to talk about but work – how uninspiring is that? There is no magic formula. Find a way that allows you to fit a bit of everything in.

Step 85

Passion

Definition:

▶ a violent emotion, eg hate, anger or envy
▶ a fit of anger
▶ sexual love or desire
▶ an enthusiasm (has a passion for bikes)
▶ something for which one has great enthusiasm (Bikes are his passion).

Chambers Concise Dictionary, 2nd edition, Chambers Harrap Publishers Ltd 2009

To be great at business transformation, you need to be passionate about it. As the definition shows it's not just about love, it's about the boundless energy and the powerful emotions that draw people to you.

Passion comes through the way you walk and talk, it radiates around an air of self-confidence that means people want to be around you.

When you are delivering change people need to come to you. Being passionate is usually inspiring and attractive, and people want to be part of it, making the journey so much easier for everyone.

You can't be passionate about something you don't enjoy. If you aren't passionate about this transformation (you are only doing it because you have to), get someone else to do it – it will be the best investment you make.

Take part in the discussion at www.cheeky-monkey.co/connect

Cheeky Monkey Wisdom

Passion has an alter ego. Passionate people get angry and they express their feelings and emotions with enthusiasm and desire. Being on the receiving end of that can feel like you have been hit by a train – be aware of that. Ask any of the Cheeky Monkeys what it's like to be on the receiving end of my passion some days!

Step 86

Courage

The greatest barrier to success is the fear of failure.

Sven Goran Eriksson

Having the responsibility for delivering business transformation or any kind of change can be the most isolating job in the world. When the going is good, there is no feeling like it, you are making a difference and it's usually very visible.

Those of you who have gone through the highs and lows of delivering change will know that you always get both and that there are usually high highs and low lows. No matter how thoroughly you try and plan everything upfront, you don't know what you don't know and things are going to go wrong. It is at that point you have a chance to go from the good to the great and all it takes is courage: the courage to say it as it is, listen and accept when you are wrong, and believe in what you are doing at any cost.

I read somewhere that the difference between courage and bravery is that courage comes from the heart. You can be brave through loyalty but you can only be courageous when it comes from a point of love. You put yourself on the line because you believe in the path you are going down and have an absolute belief that it is the right thing to do.

That doesn't mean it always is, which for people watching can be really off-putting because we don't distinguish between a courageous act that didn't work and failure that came from being scared and letting the inevitable happen – and we need to!

Courage is inspiring, contagious, attracts commitment and forms bonds between teams that become very resilient.

So when you are faced with a situation and your heart is pumping and your palms are sweaty, it's because you know there is something you need to do. Don't flee. Face it and enjoy the rewards that come with being the one with balls.

Take part in the discussion at www.cheeky-monkey.co/connect

Cheeky Monkey Wisdom

Our end-of-project review meetings are always amazing because of the journey we relive with the project team. The outpouring of emotions always centre around the big ballsy decisions we took and the elation associated with pulling it off or the pain relived as we look at why it failed. Without fail there are huge smiling faces as we pull apart the failure and without question someone will say 'I can't believe we did that!' with an overwhelming sense of pride that we had the courage to try!

Step 87

Experience

There are two sides to this topic. Experience is essential in business transformation, it's not a job for a novice and ideally you want to cut your teeth on some change projects and programmes ahead of time.

It can though make you a little narrow-minded and cause you to prejudge a situation because of your previous experiences. You can lose the ability to take a risk or see that just because you had one experience, another will follow the same path.

Experience is an advantage as long as you don't put so much value on your experience that you think you already know what it's going to take to get the job done. The moment that happens you need to step back and make sure your experience is working against what you are trying to deliver.

Take part in the discussion at www.cheeky-monkey.co/connect

Cheeky Monkey Wisdom

Getting the balance right with experience is tricky. There are so many components you will be trying to balance within your transformation: employee engagement, empowerment and distributed decision-making being key ones. To keep all those factors in play successfully you need to provide the benefit of your experience for others to evaluate and use it in the decision-making process.

Step 88

Listening

Listening is the most underused management tool we have at our disposal. Not being listened to is a soul-destroying experience that makes good people give up. Pretending to listen is the same as not listening. You can't fake it because your ears are connected to your body language and it makes you very transparent.

If you don't want to hear what someone has to say, don't ask them to talk – be honest.

When you listen to someone and they know you are listening, something amazing happens to that person. They will usually test you to see if you are really listening, and if your responses show that you are and you invite them to tell you more, they open up, physically and verbally. To be listened to seems to be such a special experience that you will always get more than you expected.

As you listen more you will start to hear the things people are trying to tell you – it's an invitation to delve deeper, take it. Usually at this stage people will open up about their ideas, or things they know will make a difference, all the things they don't normally have the courage to say, stuff you would never know if you hadn't listened.

Don't just listen to the people who you think will interest you. Listen to everyone, the people that bore you, your enemies, the cleaner (especially the cleaner, always the fount of all knowledge) – go for it. It will do good and make you feel good.

Take part in the discussion at www.cheeky-monkey.co/connect

Cheeky Monkey Wisdom

Our clients are always amazed at just how much information we get from the people they work with in a very short space of time. They ask how we do it like there is a magic formula we can give them. We put ourselves in their shoes and listen. It's magic.

Step 89

Talking

Talking does not come naturally to everyone (memories of a painfully shy childhood are proof of that). Maybe it relates to our fear of failure: there is that horrible shrinking feeling when you start talking and no one is actually listening. You can't deliver business transformation if you are not a talker and you need to be able to talk in a way that means people will listen to you.

If you are a good talker, you are usually observant. Good talkers scan the environment and open with something that ensures a reaction. They know what's going on and use that to manoeuvre the conversation to what they want to talk about.

Talking is more than giving a message or eliciting information; you can turn people's emotions by the way that you talk. You can charm them, persuade them, make them laugh (and cry), feel at ease, shock them, de-motivate and motivate them not just in what you say but how you say it. During your transformation journey you will want to do all of those things.

Saying things in the wrong way is as damaging as saying the wrong thing.

Take part in the discussion at www.cheeky-monkey.co/connect

Cheeky Monkey Wisdom

During transformation you have to keep everyone talking and you have to make sure what they are saying is worth saying and said in the right way. Working at a global level means you simplify your use of language to its purest form, otherwise you lose people. When this is happening over a conference call, it may be a week or more before you realize. Be aware of culture, and avoid the use of slang and jokes until you know people, or are at least talking to them face to face.

Step 90

Being honest

What does it mean to be honest?

Some of the definitions for honest are:

- ▶ Fair and candid in dealing with others.
- ▶ True, just, upright, trustworthy, chaste, virtuous, free from fraud and equitable.
- ▶ Honesty is characterized by openness, sincerity or being frank.

When we are tiny we are taught that telling lies is bad and we should always tell the truth. As we get older the clear line between a truth and a lie gets blurred (it's not really a lie, I just don't want to hurt their feelings, what they don't know won't hurt them, etc.) and by adulthood we know that people say things they don't mean (different to a lie). Lies are rated by the impact they have, not the fact that a lie was told. By the time we are fully fledged working adults we are resigned to the fact that people lie.

How sad is that?

When you are transforming a business, you have the fate of the business and maybe tens, hundreds or thousands of people under your control. You need to deliver that responsibility with integrity and that means being honest.

Sometimes being honest is shocking and it does upset people, normally the people that have benefited from the lies. There can be so many work-arounds put in place rather than face the truth; e.g. this system had never done what we wanted, I know but it cost £xx, we can't go back and say it doesn't work …

Following this path when delivering transformation is destructive. Getting people to be honest from the start, encouraging them to say it as they see it, is not only liberating, it will save you time and money.

Take part in the discussion at www.cheeky-monkey.co/connect

Cheeky Monkey Wisdom

One of our selling points is that we are honest. Our clients tell us that it is a USP; does that mean that everyone else is dishonest? No. We cut the crap and tell it like it is, doing that in these times is a USP. Being honest saves time, creates clarity and creates a moment of black and white in a world that has way too many shades of grey.

Step 91

Getting to know them

This is always a pause-generating question for leaders:

How much of what you get paid for is delivered by people in your team?

Generally the higher up you are in the business, the greater that proportion will be. Follow-on question:

How well do you know the people you trust that to?

You probably know them in terms of objective setting and appraisals. What about beyond that? Married? Divorced? Kids at home? Elderly parents at home? Hobbies? Do you know enough about them to understand what they really believe in and the things that affect their day-to-day thoughts and decisions?

This is not just about being nice, which should be enough of a driver; it's about you having a relationship with the people who work with you and them being able to do the same in return.

Getting to know you basics:

- ▶ Make yourself available. If you need to figure out how much time this should take, work back from the amount of work they are doing for you.
- ▶ Go for lunch with them, frequently enough so it's not an uncomfortable surprise.
- ▶ Join in conversations, talk about yourself and be interested in them.
- ▶ Talk about things that are important to you so that they understand what you believe in and value.
- ▶ Share the good and the bad.

Take part in the discussion at www.cheeky-monkey.co/connect

Cheeky Monkey Wisdom

It is easy to judge people because of the way they behave or act in different situations – all the time you build a mental picture of what that person is really like. Without knowing them it is all fantasy and most of the time wrong. Most people get up every day wanting to do the best they can that day and along the way things happen. Those things can have a huge impact on what else happens – if you know, you can help. If you don't know, you can make the situation worse without realizing.

Step 92

Inspiration

Do we need to be inspired? Nelson Mandela said 'we need inspiration because we all need to exceed our own expectations'. It's a great debate and the internet is full of people debating it.

My view is that today we are all inspired every day, we just don't always realize it. Without inspiration we would do the same thing day in, day out without trying anything new. Just think about that: you would eat, drink, dress yourself and choose a shelter only out of need not want. The majority of us are inspired to do something every day, even it's just choosing a different sandwich for lunch.

Inspiration makes us do things. It turns surviving into living.

Does the constant bombardment of messages, new things, bright lights, information, stimulation, music, words, and pictures all at an alarming speed result in us being unconsciously uninspired? We do try new things,not because we have been inspired, but because we are unconsciously uninspired and so just end up reacting to a message without emotion? E.g. I'll have that one, it will be fine, I'm not bothered.

Being unconsciously uninspired is a double negative: the opposite of being consciously inspired. Do you have to be conscious of mind to really be inspired? Take a little time out to use your senses; see, hear, touch and feel things so that they can make a difference to what you do.

We know the difference, it's just that, most of the time, we don't think we have time for the difference. Yet, as with most so-called time-saving choices we make, they end up taking longer in the end.

When you are inspired by something and give yourself a little time to think about how you are going to use that moment of inspiration and find the time to take action on it, it's like getting a turbo-charged lift to where you want to go. Things suddenly feel easier and faster to get done.

> *Life is like bicycle. To to keep your balance you must keep moving.*
>
> **Albert Einstein**

Take time out to be inspired every day. You won't need to change your routine to do this, just open yourself to the fact you are doing it. Be open and consciously inspired, and you will be amazed what a difference it will make to you and those around you.

Take part in the discussion at www.cheeky-monkey.co/connect

Cheeky Monkey Wisdom

Things that inspire us: reading, music, films, TV, friends, family, meeting and talking to strangers, art, nature, shopping, travel, games – oh, this list could go on and on.

We know that we could not hope to inspire people to deliver transformation if we ourselves weren't inspired by the things around us. We spend our days (and many of our nights) looking at how we can help achieve our clients' goals in a way that will inspire others to want to be part of it. It makes a difference to our lives, our work and the people we work with.

Step 93

Blind faith

There are lots of definitions of blind faith, none of which are what I
mean here so I need to explain first. My definition is when all is not
clear, and you are not quite sure what is going to happen and if what
you are doing is the right thing, but you need everyone to go with
you. Sometimes during transformation that is what it comes down to.
It's the ultimate show of trust by people who are intelligent enough to
know that it's probably ridiculous and counter-intuitive but they are
willing to go with it anyway. Some days you just need that.

Fostering a team spirit that allows you to get to that point is the
ultimate place to be. It not only means that you have the respect
of the team but they are also engaged in what you are all trying to
achieve and are confident enough to roll with the punches.

Take part in the discussion at www.cheeky-monkey.co/connect

Cheeky Monkey Wisdom

One of my best moments in a post-project review was listening to the team talk about things we had done in the project that required blind faith. We had become so close as a team I hadn't even realized that was what had happened in some of the examples. It was a real eye-opener to hear from those who had analysed the situation and decided how the situation would play out. Blind faith should never be confused with 'the blind leading the blind', which is in fact its opposite number (where no one really knows what is going on). Blind faith is practised by people who know what is going on but don't know what the outcome will be and have enough trust to let it play out with the confidence that it will be OK.

Step 94

Beware the hype

The hype around business transformation comes in a couple of forms:

- The excitement around what this is going to do for the business
- The buzz that is created around the people delivering the programmes and projects

People love a story. When the communication starts around the business about the transformation that we are all going to be part of, it's the start of the story. Some people just keep to the facts, say what needs to be said and leave. Others like drama: they are so good with their words that they can paint a picture for you and create real excitement about what is about to happen. Watch the line between the creation of drama and embellishment for effect.

During transformation people really listen because they are looking for any indication that this change is going to affect them personally. We are all amateur psychologists and we look for the emotional and body language indicators to confirm what we fear the most. It is unlikely that you will be able to make any guarantees at this stage; getting carried away with the 'hype' surrounding the genuine desire to engage and collaborate with your employees can lead to innocent and unfortunate problems. Someone else's perception is their reality.

It's the same when you are working on programmes and projects. You use all the 'magic' we have described to motivate, engage, listen to and get contributions from the people you are working with. If this is new behaviour, there is a cycle they go through:

- wary of reason behind the behaviour
- happy and enjoying it
- arrogant belief you can't do it without them
- angry that it's not gone all their way
- acceptance of a new way of working.

There is always a point when people think they are better than they are. You know that because you have put them there. The need is to encourage, motivate and celebrate the small stuff, and in the early days you may have to ignore some issues for the greater good: it's all positive as long as you manage the cycle. For this to be sustainable it has to get to the stage where engagement is acknowledged as both positive and negative so that everyone can become self-aware. Everybody has something to learn every day: it never stops.

Take part in the discussion at www.cheeky-monkey.co/connect

Cheeky Monkey Wisdom

Don't be put off. Working with emotionally intelligent people is rewarding on so many levels, but it can take some adjusting to and requires interpretation. It is the opposite to cold logic and clinical decision-making, where you can just tell people what to do and when they come back to you it is either right or wrong. See it as a set of new rules for an evolving game – and remember to have fun.

Step 95

Food

'Qu'ils mangent de la brioche' –not actually said by Marie Antoinette but let them eat cake is what this is all about.

It is amazing what happens when someone takes cakes into an office – it brings people together. If you have baked the cakes then another dimension is added: you look like you are warm, caring and homely, and everyone else feels strangely comforted by that.

To calm a bit of stress, to raise morale, to bond with colleagues or just for a break and a bit of fun, sharing cake can help.

The link between sharing food and trust has long been debated. When we are getting to know someone we choose to go out to dinner (personally and professionally). There is no proven link that I can find, but I believe emotional barriers lower when we eat together.

Take part in the discussion at www.cheeky-monkey.co/connect

Cheeky Monkey Wisdom

Monkey2 is our expert baker. She has won over several tough projects teams with a batch of Nigella Lawson's carrot cake muffins. She doesn't have time to be popping buns in the oven, but she recognizes the benefit of taking time out to show her team she cares.

Step 96

Playing

It can't be all work and no play can it? We spend more time with our work colleagues than we do our families and in all of that time, we're not supposed to play? It makes most of us feel better when we play at work but not all of us. We introduce playing into what we do regularly and there are some people who genuinely hate it – don't be put off by them. There are also cultural implications that you need to be aware of but not in the way you might think. The Western world is the most resistant to playing at work and the Asians the most playful (in my experience).

Sometimes there are issues that are so contentious that if you tried to sit round a table, they would never see the light of day, let alone be resolved. Trying to get different hierarchical levels to appreciate the need for behavioural change is very difficult. Truthful exchanges of what people really think are difficult, especially if different levels of hierarchy are involved. Capturing the real reasons that current processes or systems don't work, the fundamental reasons that adoption has not been realized, are hard to extract. You can make all of those things achievable by playing.

When you talk about goals, what you are trying to achieve through your transformation and the known issues that exist today to a group of people who are involved in delivering this every day they will nod, some will have a view, some may gather and share views, and a few may point out issues to their manager.

If you share that information and then ask the group of people to create a treasure map that shows the current way of working and what has to change to realize the new goals, then you start to get feedback.

Give that team some craft materials – magazines, toys, tin foil, card, straws, etc., typical children's craft cupboard items – and watch how descriptive that map becomes. Putting a toy soldier in the bushes and calling it a sniper to describe a colleague's action while presenting work at a review meeting became a relaxed moment that the team could laugh about together while getting the point across. Turning some of the hardest bits of transformation into moments when people can play together is really effective.

Take part in the discussion at www.cheeky-monkey.co/connect

Cheeky Monkey Wisdom

We use drawing a lot in exercises and without question everyone in the room will groan when we say we are going to draw. It's a leveller: no one thinks they can draw and it doesn't matter where we have been brought up in the world, we all learn to draw the same way. We all draw a house, car and person in the same way and those that don't get a chance to show how brilliant and creative they are. A picture is worth a thousand words.

Step 97

Sharing

We are social not solitary creatures: in the middle of Maslow's hierarchy of needs is our need to belong. The huge numbers of people drawn to some form of social media show that our desire to share couldn't be stronger.

Sharing is a teamwork fundamental: you divide and distribute work because together you are better and stronger.

With regard to training, you teach someone how to do a task. The best trainers share their experience and knowledge to give some context beyond the explicit instructions. The person being trained always walks away feeling like they have got more out of the training; you have given the information that allows them to start ahead of first base and that gives the person being trained confidence.

Imagine what it would do to your business if you could create a system of sharing knowledge and practice that created confidence – you can and should. Knowledge has always been power and still is, but the idea that people in the workplace can hold on to it selfishly has gone.

Training is also one of the first things that gets cut from the budget when times are hard and the shortcut when projects are running out of time. This is so short-sighted – we have to change the view of training and make it a sustainable part of the business philosophy. This can be done by focusing on the need to share.

Many businesses use coaches and mentors for the leaders in the business. This philosophy builds on the practice of mentoring and coaching throughout the business, right to grassroots. By identifying the people in your business that do things really well and formally

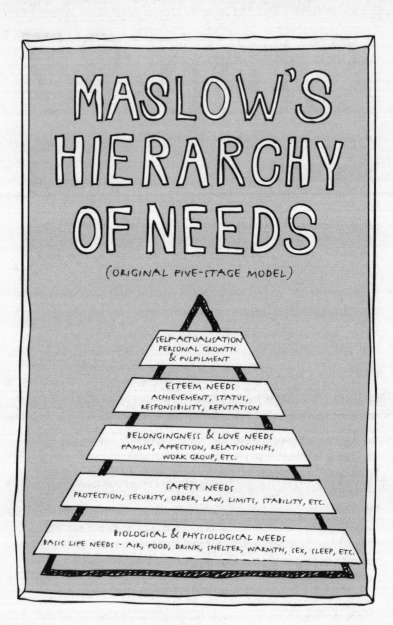

providing them with space to coach and mentor others in the business, you spread your assets positively.

It's an internal continuous improvement cycle, driven by the assets of your business. There are so many advantages to doing this I struggle to see why it isn't common practice:

▶ continuous knowledge-sharing in the business
▶ always passing on the latest thinking and/or experience
▶ easier succession planning
▶ spreads the risk – the business is not reliant on key individuals
▶ gives people purpose and creates a culture of giving back.

Look for the obvious places to start in the business; project management is usually a good one. When you look to deliver change in the business, who do you ask? It is usually a small number of people who get tasked every time: is that the place to start sharing and get a mentoring and coaching process off the ground?

Take part in the discussion at www.cheeky-monkey.co/connect

Cheeky Monkey Wisdom

One of the hardest things for us to accept is companies that watch us coach and mentor their employees, see them blossom, progress quickly, wow the crowds and then promote them and leave them with no support. In most cases those people leave the business and get better jobs elsewhere. Such a waste. Trained talent in your business needs nurturing just the same as new talent.

Step 98

Stress relief

Business transformation and delivering change can be stressful. Sometimes the sources of stress are not obvious and the little things are overlooked, leading to a meltdown moment. You need to keep an eye on this in others and yourself.

Common excuses:

▶ I have a million things to do right now, it will be better when ...
▶ Things are always crazy here.
▶ It's normal for me, I would hate it if all this wasn't going on.

The things we start to do can be common indicators of stress:

▶ smoking
▶ drinking
▶ eating
▶ not going out
▶ taking pills to relax
▶ lashing out at those around us
▶ sleeping too much
▶ not sleeping at all.

Our lives need to be balanced for us to function correctly. A combination of work, relaxation, relationships and fun is required by all of us. When we have that combination we feel like we can take on the world, we are productive and the contribution we make is significant. So why don't we keep ourselves there? Sometimes it's just not that easy and at different times we do have to dig deep when one of the components in our life requires more – that is today's reality.

Seeing the signs of that and doing something about it is important for your future health and well-being (and that of those around you).

Stress relief basics:

- ▶ Learn how to say no. Know your limits and stick to them.
- ▶ Avoid people who stress you out. If you can't, tell them they stress you out and why.
- ▶ Stop doing the things that annoy you.
- ▶ Don't get involved in repeating arguments with the same people.
- ▶ Tell people how you are feeling.
- ▶ Be willing to compromise.
- ▶ Take responsibility for your own actions.
- ▶ Be more assertive.
- ▶ Manage your time better.
- ▶ Focus on the positive.
- ▶ Look for the upside.
- ▶ Accept the world isn't perfect.
- ▶ Do something you enjoy everyday.
- ▶ Keep your sense of humour.

Take part in the discussion at www.cheeky-monkey.co/connect

Cheeky Monkey Wisdom

When you do things in the list or encourage others to do them, remember there is always another side to the situation and you may hear something you don't like. Take it constructively and act on it – don't see it as something else to get stressed about. I often encourage stress relief, which results in people assertively telling me what they are prepared to do and not to do. This is good, but when the situation you are in requires that it is done, someone has to do it, and if it's not going to be you, it needs to be someone else. Acknowledging that can be tough: don't think the world is going to stop because you need to work differently, but accept the change if it's going to relieve the stress you are under. The balanced, stress-free you is a better person.

Step 99

Thanks

Saying thanks is like smiling; it's so easy to do and makes a big difference instantly. (imagine what happens when you smile and say thank you together – initially people will think you are having a nervous breakdown and then just think you are nice.)

We all want to feel appreciated and that our contribution has made a difference, and receive positive confirmation of that from someone who matters. Reward mechanisms are great but in some places have become completely faceless. Yes, you get a card that says 'thanks' or something similar, but it still has no personal touch. If that is your system, at least write something personal in the card!

It's the personal touch that makes the difference. Going up to someone and saying thank you, shaking them by the hand or, if custom allows, giving them a hug, allows you to connect with that person's basic need to feel appreciated.

Cheeky Monkey Wisdom

We always get huge support at grassroots in the organizations we work with because we make everyone feel like they are the most important person in that business, because they are. It is always amazing the impact we have at that level and I am sure that it is because we genuinely involve everyone – we want and need the engagement of everyone and we say thank you at every step of the way. Not because we are robots and it's in our manual, but because we mean it and because what they have done has made a real difference and we want them to know that.

By the way, thanks for buying this book. I hope it's made a difference and I look forward to catching up with you at www.cheeky-monkey.co/connect. Call in for a hug anytime.

Glossary

Ambition That emotion that motivates us to do more, do it better in the hope that we are better.

Behavioural change Getting people to see the consequences of their actions. Changing areas that have a negative impact so that they have a positive one.

Blind faith When intelligent people who know what is going on but don't know what the outcome will be trust enough to let the situation play out.

Blueprint A map of the systems, processes and people that allow you to do what you do.

Business architecture The systems and processes that sit behind how you deliver the products and/or service you deliver.

Business incubator A place to nurture start-up business ideas and give them support through the early years.

Business values Beliefs that are important to the business and are used as a guide as to how they do business.

Business deliverables The tangible things (you can measure success and failure) that the business needs to deliver.

Business model The structure behind what you produce.

Business planning The stake in the ground that says this is what you are going to do, how and what it means financially.

Business transformation Joining the dots between the people, processes and systems in the organization, and the business strategy and required deliverables to take the business to its next stage.

Business-wide value perspective When you look right across the business, the things you do that keep the business alive.

Cloud computing IT delivery model based around the internet.

Cluster groups People with a common goal in different geographic locations.

Co-creating Joining forces with people who are better together.

Company silo A structure that means that people are aligned to one function in the business; their objectives, bonuses, route of progression are tied to doing well in that function – not necessarily doing well for the business.

Competitive advantage The effect of using the difference you have in the market.

Constraints Boundaries that you have to work within or around.

Culture The beliefs that people have as they go through life and are exposed to different things, e.g. social structure, religion, family, etc.

Customer insights Talking to your customers, observing what they do, encouraging feedback and looking for trends about what they are searching for.

Customer relationship management Your contacts, categorized into who they are and why they are important, and a running record of who has been in touch with them and why.

Daydream Letting your mind drift and imaging the endless possibilities that could exist.

Dependencies Tasks that need someone else or something else to be done, before or after you complete them.

Dictatorship The world view according to one person.

Differentiation Understanding what makes you different and using it.

Distributed decision-making Spreading the responsibility for making decisions and accountability for the impact throughout the business.

Ego A self-inflating emotion ('haven't I done well?') that should be enjoyed but understood for what it is.

Employee empowerment Giving employees ownership and accountability for their actions.

Facilitator A person who can direct a group of people towards a common goal without forcing their own opinions on the situation, but by getting the group to see and review all possibilities.

Food chain You need something from me to progress, I need something from Fred, he needs something from Daisy, and on we go.

Globalization A world without limits; products and services made, delivered and enjoyed as much around the world as you do at home.

Holistic Looking at the whole picture.

Hug The amazing feeling of having someone's arms around you.

Idea-to-market process The chain of events that starts with the idea for the product or service you want to deliver, right through to the product or service being in the hands of the customer.

Innovation The creation of something new.

Inspirational leader A person who people naturally follow, who is three-dimensional and cares about more than themselves.

Intellectual property Ownership of an idea or process.

Lean supply chains The cycle of supply, manufacture, delivery with all the wasteful tasks taken out.

Management initiative Strategic work that is carried out by the management team as part of their role, not 'project' work.

Marketing The communication route behind telling people about what you do.

Matrix management An attempt to break down silos without changing the organizational structure, but by giving people more than one boss: one functional and one project.

Meltdown moment When everything just becomes too much, you have lost perspective and objectivity and it all feels personal.

Mission Why you exist today.

Networked organizational structure A structure not based on hierarchy (management levels) but relationships that are required to deliver business goals.

No-brainer All the signs are positive, why wouldn't you do it?

Objectives Specific, defined elements of work that must be delivered, and success and failure can be measured. Usually SMART: Specific, Measurable, Achievable, Realistic and Time-bound.

Over-initiative era A time when starting projects in organizations is everyone's favourite pastime.

Portfolio management A way of identifying what you sell and categorizing it so you know where it stands in the market today and what the market potential for it is.

Procurement The art of buying things.

Product lifecycle management (PLM) Understanding what the lifecycles of your products and services are, managing the data associated with them effectively, collaborating with all parties, efficiently eliminating waste in the product cycle.

Programme A number of projects that link to deliver an overall business outcome.

Project A vehicle to manage change; a piece of work that has defined start and end dates, and specific deliverables that can be measured.

Project kick-off Getting all the people involved in delivery of the project together so they can discuss, debate and work through the best way of achieving what is being asked of them.

Project management Proactively managing a project to its defined conclusion. Navigating all the issues, risks and changes that will inevitably come your way.

Research and development (R&D) The people that come up with new technologies, formulations, packaging, etc.

Risk management Risks are something that may or may not happen. Managing them ensures that you keep track of the potential impact to what you are doing, hopefully before they happen.

SAAS Software As A Service allows you to access software applications on a pay-as-you-go model.

Sales and operations planning (S&OP) Linking the business plan to actual demand for your products and services and your ability to deliver.

Scope The definition of what you are going to do, i.e. what it does and doesn't include.

Steering group The people who have everything to gain or lose from the project.

Sustainability Thinking about the impact of your actions beyond what happens today.

SWOT Reviewing the Strengths, Weaknesses, Opportunities and Threats that exist in your business.

Talent management Seeing your most valuable asset as the talent pool it is. Understanding the capabilities and skills you have and making sure you nurture and develop it to its potential.

Timeline The sequence of dates that relate to when tasks need to be delivered in pursuit of a project delivery or business goal.

Value chains The tasks in the business that, when linked together, produce something of tangible value.

Venture partnerships Business partnerships that create mutual value.

Virtual working Working with people who don't sit in the same room as you.

Work-life balance Making sure you live life to the full. It's not about the amount of hours you work or when you work, just fitting a bit of everything in.

Index